HITTING THE TARGET IN SOUL WINNING

Bishop Dr. Godfrey K. Tabansi

For any information, Please contact Divine Publishers Inc.
Email: divinepublishersinc@gmail.com
www.divinepublishersinc.com

DEDICATION

This book is dedicated to the Almighty God and to:

Soul winners out there in the field laboring to harvest souls to God, and many others who tap into the secrets in this book to facilitate their work to take the whole world for Christ.

CONTENTS

ACKNOWLEDGMENTS

This book is a product of many years of my teachings and Evangelism Christian Outreach. I thank God for helping me to compile the teachings into a book, which I consider a powerful tool for evangelism. I thank God also for providing Michelle who in spite of her busy schedules found time to edit and make inputs in the book.

Special appreciation must be given to Dr. B. U Okafor

I appreciate Evangelist Michelle Walker for her full support and God's love.

PREFACE

During his three and half year ministry on earth, the Lord Jesus gave the church a prayer point that is close to his heart. It had to do with ensuring that the purpose for which he came was fulfilled. Since he was going to die for the sins of the whole world. He did not want the news of his death hidden in the corner. He needed committed workers who would go everywhere announcing this great good news to the whole world. He said, the harvest truly is great, but the laborers are few......(Luke 10-2)

Without an adequate and committed labor-force to spread the good news of Christ's death and resurrection, many sinners all over the world would still die and go to hell in spite of the fact that their salvation has already been paid for by the Lord Jesus with his precious blood. Thank God for the innumerable multitudes of saints who have had of, and who have been redeemed with the precious blood of Christ; but what about the multiplied billions of persons who are preaching even now, without knowing Christ?

And why have they not heard or known about Him? The number one reason is: The church has not been able to mobilize sufficient numbers of committed and dedicated Laborers into the harvest field to spread the good news and

salvage hell-bound souls and turn them into saints, for the kingdom of God.

If heaven rejoices over one sinner that repents and turns back to God, how much more will heaven rejoice over the saint who is instrumental to converting sinners. And will heaven not be grieved at those saints who-by failing to witness for Christ- make the precious blood of Christ unavailable to the dying world?

This is indeed real food for thought, that prayer that it will awaken even a soldier of the cross that is asleep at his duty post, to the urgent task of evangelism.

Your going today will be an answer to Christ prayer point—send forth the laborers into his harvest.

Amen.

CHAPTER ONE

THE GREAT COMMISSION

And he said unto them, Go ye into all the world, and preach the Gospel to every creature. He that believeth and is baptized shall be saved; but he that believeth not shall be damned (Mark 16:15-16).

At the close of His earthly ministry, Our Lord Jesus Christ commanded His disciples to go and preach the gospel of the kingdom to all creatures. This is one crucial assignment given to his followers to fulfill. God's heart desire is for this priority task to be carried out before the consummation of time. But this mandate of soul winning cannot be successfully carried out without a proper understanding of what it entails. A proper explanation will be of immense help.

FUNDAMENTAL EXPLANATIONS

THE GREAT COMMISSION

The great commission is a primary command issued by the Lord to every Christian to go forth and win souls into his kingdom. It involves every believer because a Christian is saved to save, saved for a witness and won to win. The Lord called us to occupy till he comes (Luke 19:13). The task is so fundamental that it has no alternative. Freedom of choice is limited to only one option - "…Go forth into the highways and hedges and compel them to come.." Luke 14:23

In summary, the Great entails:

(a) Going (taking action)
(b) Into all the world (the entire world is our field)
(c) Preach the Gospel (communicate the good news)
(d) To every creature (people of all tribes and tongues and nations).

THE COMMISSIONER

The Lord Jesus Christ issued this great command, "And Jesus came and spoke unto them, saying… Go ye therefore and teach all nations…(Math. 28:18-19). The scripture also said, "After these things the Lord appointed other seventy Also, and sent them two and two before his face into every city and place…" (LK 10:1). This command is therefore an order and not a suggestion since it flows from a superior authority – it is a well known fact that in the armed forces, you dare not disobey superior commands. The worry in this is that men are careful to obey and follow through when it has to do with earthly authority but can easily ignore an order from the Almighty God.

However, the scripture confirms that the early saints were obedient to this call, "The Lord gave the word: great was the company of those that published it." (ps. 68:11) By this every believer has a non-negotiable mandate to go about the business of soul winning to bring in a harvest unto the Lord. It is the heartbeat of the Almighty God, and should not, for any reason, be ignored. In fact Jesus bluntly said if we do not gather with him, then we are scattering. (Matt. 12:30)

THE COMMISSINED

The Lord is the commissioner and we are the commissioned. Even a genuine believer is called to witness, "…Go ye into all the world and preach the gospel to every creature." (MK 16:15) There is no exception! People of all trade and professions – we are involved whether we are traders, farmers, teachers, apprentices, doctors, lawyers, Pastors or businessmen. It does not even matter whether we are educated or not. In the scripture "unlearned and ignorant fisher men were called. Matt 4:1 1, Acts 4;13) You and I are vessels God is relying on to accomplish the Great Commission. Jesus had told the crowd which tried to stop those who were shouting, "Hosanna to the Highest" at the triumphant entry into Jerusalem that if they succeeded in silencing them that he would cause stones to raise and declare the works of God. It will be unfortunate if in our days God would employ stones to do what He has commissioned us to do. When the early saints headed this call the Church grew in leaps and bounds. The Great Commission is a "growing concern". The early Church knew this fact and became a going Church and expectedly a growing Church developed. Today, the complacent attitude of believer and our "arm chair" Christianity is breaking the heart of our God. When one has been genuinely and graciously redeemed, one cannot but need this great call. The greatest demand has always been for believers to heed this ageless call of stepping out and winning souls unto the Lord. Heaven is waiting for the response.

THE MESSAGE OF THE COMMISSION

The encapsulated in this call is a message of love. To go forth and preach the gospel is to declare the good news. It is not just any news but the "good news". It is a message of hope that is born out of Love. ...(God is not) willing and that any should perish, but that all should come to repentance." (II Pet. 3:9) It is a message of forgiveness not a message of condemnation. Every body feels good to hear that he/she is loved. That is exactly what God is saying to us in the gospel, we are therefore asked to go out and tell sinners their need of a Saviour. This is because if they do not repent of sin, they are lost. As guilty sinners, they will be judged. (Rom 3: 10-23) Therefore, we must let them know the truth of God's judgement and punishment and God's love resulting in the provision of the Saviour Jesus Christ. (Jn 3:16).

GOD'S LOVE FOR SOULS

Every child of God ought to know why this commission is the Lord's heartbeat. God gave his best and highest to consummate this. Yes, "God so loved the world, that he gave his only begotten son that whosoever believeth in him should not perish, but have everlasting life." (Jn 3:16) God's heart is always bleeding whenever he beholds men toying with this supreme assignment for which he gave his best---imagine God leaving his heavenly mansion, taking the form of mortal man. Imagine Jesus suffering and dying on the cruel cross of Calvary for salvation of all mankind; in spite of this, men are still winning and dinning instead of stepping out of their comfort zone to declare the good news.

The call of the Great Commission is motivated by the Lord's passion to see the lost saved. It is concern to get souls saved that compelled Jesus to die on the cross for our salvation. Human souls are of great value to the Lord God. This is why he paid the highest price with his son. Should we then continue to ignore this great call, this love for which the Lord has paid the ultimate price?

THE REQUIREMENT OF THE COMMISSION

The Great Commission carries some fundamental requirements. The commissioned must be born again. God cannot afford to entrust this vital task to the unsaved; How can one talk of a savior he does not know? Part of the problem today is that many in our churches are not yet genuinely converted and so do not understand the essence of the commission. To partake in the Great Commission, the fellow must have the power of attorney – the legal right to use the name of Jesus. The seven sons of Sceva who tried to preach and cast out devil, suffered a public shame for trying to use the name of Jesus whom they did not know. (Acts 19:14-16)

Again, one must know the word of God or at least the message of the commission to be able to face the challenges involved. We must study to show ourselves approved unto God, workmen that need not to be ashamed, rightly dividing the word of truth (2 Tim 2:15). We the commission must also maintain regular communion with God, the commissioner, through prayer without which we nothing. Furthermore, holy living and Holy Ghost baptism are required for effective fulfillment of the commissioned.

THE CHALLENGES OF THE COMMISSION

The harvest is already "white" and further delay could be dangerous. We are at the Zero hour. A man whose house is on fire cannot afford to be busy with trivial matter. The Great Commission is the Lord's business and it requires urgency. (I Sam 21:8) "say not ye, there are yet four months, and then cometh harvest? Behold, I say unto you lift up your eyes, and look on the fields; for they are white already to harvest" (Jn 4:35) The harvest is now; the harvest is plenteous but the laborers are few.(Matt 9:37)

THE URGENCY

The harvest is ripe and wasting. Multitudes of people are streaming to hell on a daily basis. Majority of these people have not heard the gospel and average life—span on earth is short. Statistics (obtained year ago) have shown that 9,916 people die every hour, over 238,00 die every day, and about 87 million people die every year all over the world. (source: W.F. Kumuyi; Have Compassion on Them p. 57) Now think of the alarming events in the world today. How many are dying are even this minute? Billions are dying and hurrying to eternity without Christ and how much do we care for their souls? Millions that are still alive will likewise perish unless we rise up to do something now. Eternity is endless. Souls lost can never be recovered! Every unsaved soul is like perishable commodity. Please let us rise up now and witness to the lost!

THE VAST UN-REACHED FIELD

The command is to preach the good news to every creature…" unto the uttermost parts of the earth" (Matt 28:18-20; Mk 16: 15-16) There are no geographical limits, no political boundaries, no class distinctions or racial discrimination. Our mission field is vast—beginning from our neighborhoods, cities, towns, streets, remote villages, foreign lands, etc. Many of these areas are yet uncovered with effective gospel work. This vast size of un-reached people and land calls for a large workforce. But the laborers are few. As we take s close look at our Jerusalem (neighborhood), can we say, of a truth, that they are fully evangelism? The right thing to do is to enlist in the end time army of harvesters in order to carry the gospel to all these un-reached places before the close of this age. We must remember also that we are saved to serve. Do not count yourself out, thinking that evangelism is for others. It is for you as well. The world is willing to see the "Apostle Pauls" of this generation. Many communities are yet to hear and see the light of this glorious gospel. They are waiting for you. They are waiting for us.

COUNTER EVANGELISM

Human souls are precious to God (Matt 16:26), and the devil knows this very well. That is why he does his best to counter the efforts made towards winning these souls to the Lord. As we labor to win souls the devil also labors to make his own converts. He tries to turn away the faith of many from the gospel. This can be understood if we remember the activities of Bar—Jesus the false prophet who tried to stop the Deputy(governor) of Antioch(Sergius Paulus from receiving the gospel when Paul and Barnabas were preaching. (Acts 13:7-8) Today, there are many false prophets and teachers preaching a counterfeit gospel.

We live in a time when known occultist institutions are transforming over night into "Living Churches" and are fast making converts. Cults and all forms of secret societies are on the increase in our society and institutions of higher learning. The devil knows that the time is short. This is why he maximizes, every opportunity he gets to rush men to hell. (Rev.12:12) Millions of unsaved souls are being detained and destroyed by the enemy. Powers of darkness are expanding the scope of their evil activities more than ever before. There is an increasing tide of violence, bloodshed, killing, arsons and immorality in the world. Diseases that have never been known before are now on rampage. Today you hear about Acquired Immune Deficiency Syndrome(AIDS), Severe Acute Respiratory Syndrome(SARS) and other deadly diseases fashioned by the devil to hasten the departure of souls of men into hell. It is high time we plundered and liberated men already imprisoned by the devil.

THE IMMINENT RETURN OF THE LORD
There is no gain saying the fact that we are living in the last days. The end of the world is near; the coming of the Lord is imminent. Yet not much has been done. The Happenings in contemporary times are pointers to the fact that the Lord will soon come. Most of the prophecies concerning His return are all coming to fulfillment before our eye. Jesus said, "And this gospel of the kingdom shall be preached in all the world for a witness unto all nations; and then shall the end come." (Matt 24-14) The time is short. We need to rise up and do the work of evangelism

before it is too late. We can only work while it is still day; the night is coming when no man will be able to work.

THE POWER OF THE GOSPEL

The gospel has the power to liberate and set men free from bondage on earth. Paul called it the power of God unto salvation. It is the sharpest known sword, the mightiest sledge hammer and the greatest chain breaker . This "power" is released only when we preach the gospel. The gospel we preach is a power-carrier. The clarion call to the Great Commission is a call to demonstrate the power of God. The scripture says, "as ye go, preach…heal the sick, cleanse the lepers, raise the dead, cast out devils: freely ye have received, freely give." (Matt 10: 7-8) The gospel transforms lives and changes things. We should never be afraid to preach it. It is a big privilege to be honored with the responsibility of preaching the gospel.

This power of the gospel makes Christianity real and differentiates it from any other religion.

CONSEQUENCES OF NEGLECT

The price of neglecting this great task is grave. Sinners are waiting to be saved and believers have what they need to spread the good news. Failure to step out and preach the gospel amounts to a deliberate act of negligence on our part and this is very serious. God would not take that from us. Neglect is costly. It is like a man hearing that his house is on fire and yet he does nothing. There is no doubt that such a man will suffer loss. He will definitely have questions to answer before God on the day of Christ!

Other consequences of neglect of the Gospel:

CLOSED DOORS

To ignore the Lord's Command is a sin of disobedience. Sin is one thing that quickly shuts the heavens against a man. Many Christians may be operating under closed heaven because they have left the work of the Lord undone. The neglect of God's work hinders prayers and hinders progress. (Prov. 21:13) Jonah was taught the lesson of his life in the belly of a fish when he disobeyed the call to go to Nineveh and preach. Are you ignoring the call to preach in your Nineveh (neighborhoods, cities, towns and villages, etc?)

IT ATTRACTS CURSES

Failure to do the work of the Lord may attract curses. The people of Meroz were cursed bitterly by the angel of the Lord. (Judges 5:23) What was their offence? They refused to come to the help of the Lord when they were needed. When the call was made they did nothing and their idleness landed them into trouble.

ABSENCE OF PEACE

Failure to preach Christ to others can also make one lose his peace of mind. A believer who refuses to preach to save souls from going to hell is practicing mischief. "There is no peace for the wicked," says the Lord.

DANGERS OF ETERNAL JUDGEMENT

Firstly, anyone who knows the truth and refuses to preach it comes under the judgement of God. "If thou forbear to deliver them that are drawn unto death, and those that are ready to be slain: if thou sayest, Behold, we knew it not: doth not he that pondereth the heart consider it? And he that keepeth thy soul, doth not he know it? And shall not he render to every man according to his works" (Prov 24: 11-12) The Lord expressly warned the Church through his prophet, Ezekiel saying: "Son of man, I have made thee a watchman…therefore hear the word at my mouth, and give them warning from me. When I say unto the wicked, thou shalt surely die: and thou givest him not warning nor speakest to warn the wicked from the wicked way, to save his life: the same wicked man shall die in his iniquity: but his blood will I require at thine hand. (Ezek. 3:17-18) God holds us responsible for failing to show sinners the only way out of sin. Jesus Christ the first born from the dead is the only way to salvation.

Secondly, if we fail to preach the gospel we may fail to shine as stars in Christ's Kingdom: "And they that be wise shall shine as the brightness of the firmament; and they that turn many to righteousness as the stars forever and ever." (dan 12:3)…he that winneth souls is wise(Prov 1 1:30).

THE TIME IS NOW

We must do something now or never. Two thousand years after the light of salvation came to us, billions of people are still in darkness. The field is ripe and ready for harvest, but many believers are still living as if nothing is at stake, God is calling us all to go out urgently for his work. "whom shall I send? Who shall go for us?" Heaven is amazed that Christians are not ready to do the work—the work that cost God his only begotten son. God has given His best for the souls of men to be saved. How do we feel seeing these precious souls dying without Christ? How long will we remain unruffled and unconcerned about the fate of the Multitude rushing to hell every day? Will you not join the rescue team of soul winners to minimize the Lord's losses? The Great Commission is an opportunity in a life time. God needs you and now is the time!

CHAPTER TWO

VISION FOR SOULS

A soul winner must have vision for souls to be able to witness more effectively. A man of vision they say, is a man on a mission. The bible, on its part, reechoed this truth: "Where there is no vision, the people perish…" (Prov 29:18) Vision dictates our direction. The much we can see is the much we can accomplish. Clarity of vision brings clarity of action. Men who dream and have insight into the spiritual, men who see farther than others. In all ages, God reckons with such people. Men who have visions for souls see things the way God sees them. God confirmed Jeremiah's vision—"Moreover the word of the LORD came unto me, saying, Jeremiah what seest thou? I said, I see a rod of an almond tree. Then said the Lord unto me, thou hast well seen: for I will hasten my word to perform it." (jer 1:11-12). Without a proper vision for evangelism, souls will continue to perish in their multitudes in hell. But God is interested in redeeming the human soul. It is the only thing that will return to Him(God) at the end of life. A vision has been defined as "an expression of faith in a dream revealed by God for the purpose of fulfilling a mission that carries with it a burden and blessing" (Dr. S. S. Ogan) Vision for souls therefore, is a dream, an insight and understanding of the worth of human souls and burden to do something towards their salvation.

We shall now examine the value of a soul in relation to our definition of what constitutes vision in order to bring out the reason why we must have vision for human souls:

VALUE OF A HUMAN SOUL

For what is a man profited, if he shall gain the whole world, and lose his own soul? Or what shall a man give in Exchange for his soul? (Matt. 16:26):

More than the whole world. The above scripture quoted gives us an insight into the value of a soul. A man's soul will be worth more to him (and to us) than the whole world put together. In other words, a man who gains the whole world and loses his soul is still a loser. The value of the human soul cannot be measured in monetary or material terms. It cannot be exchanged for anything. Yet men spend their time more on things that are of much lesser value than the soul of man.

People invest so much time, energy and money to acquire expertise in one field of human endeavor or the other. It is obvious that human expertise put together can never be too great, no humiliation too deep, no suffering too severe or labor too hard in the effort to save a human soul.

GOD GAVE CHRIST JESUS—HIS HIGHEST AND BEST GIFT

God placed such a high premium on the human soul that he found no substitute to send in the redemption of man than his only begotten son, Jesus Christ. He paid as much as Jesus Christ to buy us back. "For God so loved the world, that He gave his only begotten son, that whosoever believeth in Him should not perish, but have everlasting life. (Jn 3:16) God's heart breaks whenever he sees the huge investment he made by giving his only begotten son wasting. This is the reason why he instituted the Great Commission. This should make to win souls into God's Kingdom.

MAN IS CREATED in His image. God attaches much importance to human souls because He made man in His own image. (Gen 1:26-29) God intended to make us as gods on earth dominating in all sphere of life.

God has done all He should to have His image—the human soul, the beauty of His Creation—to be in heaven with Him no wonder He issued a mandate to us on the ministry of reconciliation. "And all things are of God, who hath reconciled us to Himself by Jesus Christ, and hath given to us the ministry of reconciliation." (2 Cor 5:18)

JOY IN HEAVEN

Have you imagined what causes the greatest joy in Heaven? Unspeakable joy is experienced in Heaven when a single soul repents. We know that heaven is a place of joy, but there is no other place in the Bible that it is openly mentioned that there is special joy in heaven except when a sinner repents. What happens is that whenever a sinner repents and turns to God, he recoups part of his investment and heaven has every cause to be joyful. God love souls and has done everything to save mankind, "Greater love hath no man than this, that a man lay down his life for his friend(Jn 15:13) What a great privilege and honor that a soul will make the almighty God happy!

BATTLE FOR A HUMAN SOUL

God is interested in man's redemption and likeness. Satan also is interested in human souls and that is why he did all he could (though in vain) to stop the plan of salvation provided by God through Christ. Jesus came to destroy the works of Satan and liberate man from every captivity. In an attempt to stop the salvation plan. Satan used Herod to eliminate children from two years old and under (matt 2:16), about when Jesus was born, Satan hates the human soul and will do anything to ruin and destroy the soul. The ferocity of the devil's attack on mankind is an index of the worth of the human soul. He blinds the eyes of the people lest the should see the light of the glorious gospel and repent. The scripture describes clearly the mindset of those who reject the gospel: "…the god of this world hath blinded the minds of them which believe not, lest the light of the glorious gospel of Christ, who is the image of God should shine unto them." (2 Cor 4:4). The devil uses many strategies to lead souls astray. In the garden of Eden, he made Adam and Eve to doubt what God had commanded. (Gen 3:1) He always downplays the seriousness of losing one's soul in Hell. He makes people not to believe that life is short. He deceived the foolish rich man to think that he had a much longer time to live and enjoy his wealth. Said the rich fool: "… I will say to my soul, thou hast much goods laid up for many years: take thine ease, eat, drink, and be merry." (Lk 12:19). All these receiving strategies are Satan's efforts to damn the souls of men in hell. What we are willing to suffer or sacrifice in order to save souls indicates the value we place on human souls.

GOD'S VISION FOR MAN

God's original plan for man is to have unbroken fellowship and relationship with him at all times. He made Adam and Eve and placed them in the beautiful garden of Eden. But this bliss did not last long as man sinned and thereby broke fellowship with God. Man lost the glory. (Ron 3:23)

In his foreknowledge, God had initiated a plan for man's redemption. God said, "And I will put enmity between you the and woman, and between thy seed and her seed; it shall bruise thy head and thou shall bruise his heel." (Gen 3:15)

The vision to save or recover lost souls was God's idea. "For the son of man is come to seek and save that which was lost." (Lk 19:10). The scripture describes Jesus, the Son of God as, "… the lamb slain from the foundation of the world.: (Rev 13:8) These scriptures reveal the importance God attaches to the human soul. God had to give His dear Son because He could neither use Angels nor the blood of animals to redeem man. It is only the blood of His Son that was considered worthy to redeem man. What a great vision, for, 'neither the blood of goats or calves, but by His own blood He entered in once into the holy place having obtained eternal redemption for us. (Heb. 9:12)

After this costly price was paid at Calvary God's vision for man did not stop. The vision for souls is like a relay race. God handed the baton to Jesus who also handed it over to the disciples. The Lord commanded his disciples to go and preach to the whole world. God is not willing that any soul should be lost. (2 Pet. 2:9) The vision for souls is very reason why we are left on earth after our conversion.

Nothing pleases God more than seeing this vision out by believers to get souls in the kingdom God.

Again, if we appreciate the deplorable staff of sinner, we will be stirred up to go win sinners back to God.

THE DEPLORABLE STATE OF A SINNER
a) A sinner is a debtor needing pardon. (Col. 2:13)
b) A Sinner is a rebel needing reconciliation. (Rom 5:10)
c) A sinner is a criminal needing justification (Rom 3:19-25)
d) A sinner is a slave needing redemption (Jn 8:34)
e) A sinner is lost needing salvation (Lk 19:10)
f) The sinner is dead needing regeneration (Eph 2:1)

The unsaved is in a pitiable state. He has no hope. He is daily under the hope of his task master the devil. Sinners have lost consciousness of where they are going. Deep down in the heart of most of them is a desire to be free, but they do not know how to break free from Satan's chains. They are living in divers kinds of sins and if nothing is done they will perish in hell. Except we see the need to have the multitude around us saved, we can never evangelize. It was God's vision for lost sinners that made Him to send Jesus. "For when we were yet without strength, in due time Christ died for the ungodly. For scarely for a righteous man will one die; yet peradventure for a good man some would even dare to die. But God commendeth his love towards us, in that while we were yet sinners Christ died for us." (Rom. 5:6-8)

It is important to note that the ungodly are sinful, depraved, ruled and enslaved by Satan. But God has given every sinner the hope of salvation. Every sinner is bent on following his own destructive way, but God very graciously provided a way out. Sinners are enemies of the cross, haters of God and opposers of the truth but in due time God provided a way of escape.

DEEP COMPASSION FOR THE LOST

We must ask God for a burning Christ-like desire to reach out to the lost for the salvation of their souls. Where there is compassion there will be a clear vision, a burden and urgency in the heart to do something about the state of the wicked and their eventual fate. Today instead of asking what is wrong with the sinner, we should ask what is wrong with our hearts. A dry, cold insensitive and unconcerned heart will do nothing but sit down and watch sinners in their multitudes perishing in hell. Compassion is the principal factor that moved Christ to die for us! We ought to pray earnestly that this mind be found in us. Are we not challenged that multitudes around have not had the gospel? The plea of the rich man who saw unbearable agony and torments in hell should move our heart (Lk 16:19-31)
It should stir up compassion in the heart of any genuine Christian towards the lost. Deep compassion is the propelling force that moves men to evangelism.

THE INEVITABLE END OF SINNERS

The wages of sin is death. (Rom 6:23) The inevitable consequences of living without God is the loss of one's soul in hell. Hell is a place of torment and suffering where the lost souls are punished without end. The vision and mission of every believer should be to rescue souls from going to hell. "But the fearful, and unbelieving, and the abominable, and murderers, and idolaters, and all liars, shall have their part in the lake which burneth with fire and brimstone which is the second death." (Rev. 21:8)

CONCLUSION

Show me a penny whose image and superscription hath it? They answered and said Caesar's. And he said unto them, "Render therefore unto Caesar the things which he Caesars's and unto God the things which he God's." (Lk 20:24-25)

A proper vision to redeem lost souls who are making a steady advance to hell is compulsory for every Christian. It is optional. God's vision for man did not terminate with Jesus dying on the cross of Calvary. Neither did it end when Jesus resurrected and ascended into heaven. His ultimate plan and purpose is that (if possible) all human souls will come back to Him in Heaven through the furnished work at Calvary. God's heart bleeds whenever human soul ends up in hell. Heaven rejoices whenever He recovers part of His own image the human soul. Man is God's highest creation. He is the image and glory of God... (1Cor 11:7)

Prior to the end of Christ Ministry on earth, He handed over to us the Great Commission to ensure that God's ultimate vision for lost souls is not interrupted. (Mk 16:15) Therefore, our vision for souls is rightly an extention of authoritative command and mandate to "go and preach the gospel to every creature". It is the supreme task. It is God's heart beat. We have been given the ministry of reconciliation. "And all things are of God, who hath reconciled us to himself by Jesus Christ and hath given to us the Ministry of Reconciliation (2 Cor 5:18) Let us endeavor to fulfill this great ministry that is so precious to God.

CHAPTER 3

THE QUALITIES OF A SOULWINNER

In this chapter, we will look at the qualities of a soulwinner: But before that, let us take a brief look at the words of Some prominent soulwinners

> Let the cross be raised again at the centre of the market place, as well as on the steeple of the church. Jesus was not crucified in a cathedral between two candles but on the cross between two thieves (T.L. Osborne).

> Give me a hundred men who love God with their hearts and fear nothing but sin, and I will move the world (John Wesley).

> It is enough for the disciple that he be as his mater, and the servant as his lord...(Jesus Christ, Mathew 10:25).

Soulwinning is every believer's ministry. There are no spectators or bench warmers as far as the work is concerned. However, God is looking for willing and capable people who can do the work effectively. The right men rather than the best methods are needed. God is seriously in need of a crack team of soulwinners that will plunder hell, release Satan's captives and populate heaven with precious souls. The fact that the harvest is plenteous, "already white" and wasting is not in doubt. The problem staring us in the face is how to secure more willing and capable laborers. Little wonder, the Master of the harvest asked us to make this request: "Pray ye therefore the lord of the harvest, that he will send forth laborers will do the harvesting with much result. To engage in the Great Commission without quality soulwinners could be likened to trying to cut grass in the field with blunt knives. You will labor so much and achieve so little!

Now Let us look at some of essential qualities of an effective soulwinner:

GENUINE CONVERSION

Apostle Paul, a missionary and soulwinner, while writing to Timothy, stated the obvious when he said, "The husbandman that laboureth must first be the partaker of the fruits" (2 Timothy 2:6).

As a first and necessary step, every soulwinner must have tasted the very sweet fruit he is giving to others. This should be evident in his lifestyle. By that we mean, he must have a genuine testimony of salvation. Nothing short of this is acceptable. Otherwise, how can one talk of a salvation he has not encountered? A blind man cannot appreciate the beauty of colors, neither can a man without experience of spiritual rebirth be a witness for Christ. It is only when one is born again that he will have something to share with sinners. An unconverted soul witnessing to another is like a blind man trying to lead another blind man. The result? Both blind men will definitely fall into a ditch. The born again experience is not theoretical but practical and experiential.

A life dedicated to Jesus Christ will always have something to share with sinners. Even the testimony of salvation could suffice to convict a sinner. This is exactly what the Samaritan woman did when she ran into the city. She invited people to come and see the man who told her all she ever did. A soulwinner's major work is to rescue souls going to hell, which an unsaved person cannot do. Only a skillful, dedicated, compassionate Christian can do this. Therefore, mere church-attendance cannot qualify any person to become a witness for Christ. He must be born again.

A true knowledge of the Lord coupled with a sound understanding of the word of God is the mark of an effective soulwinner. One cannot give what one does not have. If we have the word of God dwelling richly in us, and we are obedient to the word, then we shall have more of Christ nature, and be able to give His living Word to others. A student who fails to prepare for an examination has prepared to fail. Likewise, a soulwinner who refuses to diligently study the word of God will not be able to witness effectively. Paul advised Timothy, the young evangelist, thus: "Study to show theyself approved unto God, a workman that needeth not to be ashamed, rightly dividing the word of truth" (2 Timothy 2:15). A sound knowledge of the word is very important. It enables a soulwinner to know the appropriate word to use. It also helps him to handle questions and objections wisely. Finaly, it helps him to lead a sinner to make a decision for Christ.

Using the right scriptures at the right time during witnessing is like a sharp surgical knife in the hand of a skilled surgeon in the theatre. It can do wonders. A soulwinner therefore must never assume that he knows what to say at every opportunity or that he has no need to study the word of God. There is so much study.

Seemingly familiar scriptures that the illumination of the Holy Spirit could reveal. In one of our evangelism outings, a Christian brother was almost embarrassed by an inquisitive sinner he was witnessing to until another brother who had the word came to his rescue and eventually led the same person to Christ. Sinners are of different categories; and some are very intelligent and argumentative. Soulwinners must therefore have the word so as to be able to witness to them effectively. A good knowledge of the word is necessary, for example, to witness to Jehovah's Witness and Catholics.

PRAYER POWER

A committed soulwinner must also be a prayer warrior. This is because there is much opposition against evangelism which will only be subdued by aggressive prayers. Sincere and serious prayers simplify the process of soulwinning. Fervent prayers born out of burden and concern for the unsaved before witnessing bring quick conviction in their hearts. Prayer softens the heart of the unsaved; it breaks barriers and provides open doors of witnessing to soulwinner. Prayer draws a soulwinner closer to the vine (Jesus Christ) without whom we can do nothing (John 15:5). It is impossible for one to witness victoriously without living prayerful life. The Lord said, "Ask of me, and I shall give thee the heathen for thine inheritance, and the uttermost parts of the earth for thy possessions" (Psalm 2:8).

A Christian brother once testified how he went out to preach and entered into a house not knowing that the house belonged to an occultist. While he was witnessing to the other members of the household, the man came in suddenly. Then he angrily locked the door, took a piece of chalk, drew a circle on the floor. Having done that, without saying a word, he began making some incantations intending to deal with the brother. Unfortunately for him, the brother was a prayer warrior. On noticing this, he went into violent prayers and the occultist became afraid and rushed to open the door to let him go. The evil man thought he had gotten a prey for rituals not knowing the he was putting his hands into fire. A soulwinner must pray very well before stepping out to witness.

Finally, the soulwinner must pray earnestly because the sinner is in Satan's bondage, and only the power of God can set him free. Jesus said that no man can go into the house of a strongman. Satan is a strongman but through Christ we can bind him and release his prisoners! Amen.

LIFE OF HOLINESS

Holy living is indispensable in evangelism. In this, Jesus remains our model in soulwinning. He lived an impeccable life in this corrupt world. The devil could not find anything to accuse Him of. When a soulwinner lives in sin, Satan will seal his lips and he would not be able to proclaim the word of God effectively. One committed Christian believer once confessed that when he fell into sin of sexual immorality, spiritual adultery, stealing and bearing false witness, he could hardly preach for months. The devil sealed his lips and tormented him with guilt. This is what the devil always does to any careless soulwinner.

When we live a holy life, we attract the presence and power of God to witness effectively. As channels through which God can communicate His message to a dying world, a soulwinner must live right. Corrupt living corrodes and contaminates the message. Once a soulwinner begins to meddle with sin, people will no longer take his message seriously. Holiness in life and conduct should be our daily experience as holy living is vital for fruitful evangelism. In 2 Timothy 2:21, the Bible says, "if a man therefore purge himself from these, he shall be a vessel unto honor, sanctified, and meet for the master's use, and prepared unto every good work."

SPIRIT-FILLED LIFE

Loving a Spirit-filled life is another imperative for successful soulwinning: Evangelism is a battle to snatch souls from Satan's prison and plan them In God's kingdom. It is a war that cannot be waged with carnal weapons. Satan is always set to defeat and disgrace any "soldier" who is not empowered by the Holy Spirit. A Spirit-filled Christian is an effective soulwinner. The Holy Ghost emboldens him to preach the gospel. He leads him on how to evangelize and goes ahead of him to prepare the work in the field. It is the Holy Spirit that convinces and convicts a sinner. Only the Holy Spirit can bring a sinner to repentance and salvation. A spirit-filled believer is endowed with Spirit-filled life, the fruits of the Spirit will manifest. These fruits are necessary ingredients for successful soulwinning.

COMPASSION

Compassion is a key factor in soulwinning We either have it and succeed or neglect it and fail. A burning Christ-like burden and concern to reach out to the lost for their salvation is the evidence of a compassionate heart. It is a driving force that moves us to witness. It enables a soulwinner to see the way God sees and know the horrible state of the unsaved. It will make a soulwinner appreciate the shortness of time and the urgency of the work. It arouses in a soulwinner a vision for the souls of men. The index of our compassion may be measured by hardship we endure, sacrifices we make, the fervent prayers we offer, the tears we shed and the earnest invitation to Christ we give to the souls of men. A person who lacks compassion may see multitudes of unsaved souls around him dying and yet do nothing. Except there is compassion to stir up the needs around us, we can never evangelize. In Acts 16:9-10, Paul was able to respond to the Macedonian call without delay because his heart was filled with compassion.

WISDON

Wisdom is a potent tool in soulwinning which soulwinners must possess. Many souls have escaped our grip due to lack of wisdom. The soulwinner must be wise in his presentation of the gospel. Wisdom is the principal thing: therefore get wisdom (Proverbs 4:7). In Mathew 10:16, the Lord underscored the importance of wisdom in soulwinning:

"Behold, I send you forth as sheep in the midst of wolves:

be ye therefore wise as serpents, and harmless as dove."

This scripture implies that we need to possess the wisdom superior to that of our enemy before we can out wit him in the battle for human souls. In the field of play, footballers and coaches study the past matches of their opponents to know their strategies. Watching the opposing team play also reveals the weakness and strengths of the individual players and the team as a whole. In like manner, soulwinners must note the strategy (wisdom) of the devil before going out to defeat him in the battle for souls. A wise soulwinner knows what to do at the right time. He knows how to approach a sinner, what to say, how to manage his time and when to conclude the message. A preacher once told us how he attended a wedding ceremony where the preacher delivered a wonderful sermon but lacked wisdom. He stretched the message for over two hours. At the end of the message the audience was so bored and tired that they heaved a sigh of relief and made an alter call, no single soul came out to surrender his life to Christ. All the sinners in the gathering had gone. He failed to walk in wisdom toward them that are without (Colossians 4:5) Holy boldness comes from the Holy Ghost. A witness must be bold to preach and bold to exercise faith in the God of miracles. Such a bold soulwinner remembers that Jesus is still alive to deliver.

SENSE OF MISSION

An active soulwinner is one who has received the commission—the "responsibility" to preach and is on a mission. He has heard the call to the Great Commission. Such people hazard their lives for the sake of the gospel. Such men can say with Paul in I Corinthians 9:16, "…for necessity is laid upon me: yea, woe is unto me, if I preach not the gospel!"

LIVING OUT THE MESSAGE

Effective and quality soulwinner must be able to live out the message they preach. Their lives must be a visible testimony of their message. Once a soulwinner begins to live a life marked by double standards, credibility will be eroded. People will no longer take his message seriously. A suspicious lifestyle can destroy a soulwinner';s message. This must have informed the words of Paul to the Romans: Thou Therefore which teachest another, teachest thou not thy self? Thou that preaches a man should not steal, doest thou steal? Thou that sayest a man should not commit adultery doest thou commit adultery? Thou that abhorest idols, does thou commit sacrilege... For the name of God is blasphemed among the Gentiles through you, as it is written...(Romans 2:21-22, 24)

A song writer summarized Paul's message to soulwinners this way:

> "If I preach the gospel to the world and fail to do same, I suffer now the shame..."

FAITH AND PERSERVERANCE

A committed witness must have faith and perseverance. Such a person would not easily give up over a sinner's refusal or reluctance to give his life Christ. He has faith that with God all things are possible and is not discouraged by initial set backs.

Without faith and perseverance, the work could be abandoned half-way. This could happen when the expected response is not coming. Men of faith and perseverance believe God for the salvation of the unsaved and work with patience and doggedness even when there are no immediate visible results. Again, difficulties, trails, persecutions and setbacks will not discourage them. This is why the Apostle Paul could say in the misdst of bonds and afflictions, "But none of these things move me…" (Acts 20:24). Faith and perseverance will bring sustainability in the time of difficulty.

WINSOMENESS

An effective soulwinner must have an attractive and cheerful personality. He must be polite in opening up a discussion with the unsaved. Lake of courtesy can close the door of the gospel. Frowning of faces can scare the unsaved. Trained and experienced soulwinners will politely win souls and follow them up. The job of the Lord is their strength!

VISION FOR SOULS

One thing that marks out the committed soulwinner from others is the vision for the souls of men. He understands the worth of a human soul. He bears in mind what it cost God to save man and understands the present state of the unsaved and the terrible punishment that awaits any soul without Christ. Today, we have many preachers who have "vision for material things and money" but not for souls. A minister wanted his pastor friend to help him organize a crusade but was sorely disappointed by his friend's reaction. His friend's concern was for money. Said he, "My rule is that any day I preach, it is five thousand dollars." If I preach for four days it is twenty thousand dollars." Is this not merchandising the gospel and the gift of God in us? This preacher has lost the vision for the souls of men, and developed a vision for mammon. May God have mercy on us.

MEN WITH A RIGHT MOTIVE
Any committed soulwinner should have but one motive— to win souls unto the Lord. Such people preach nothing but Christ. They see themselves as unworthy servants and seek only to please their Master. Many preachers lack the right motive. They seek their own glory instead of the glory of God. Some preach to make money; others preach for fame, and others preach for some other reasons. They are not gathering with the Lord but they are gathering for themselves.

KNOWLEDGEABLE IN CURRENT AFFAIRS
There is a saying that knowledge is power. A good soulwinner therefore must be abreast with current and social issues. This gives him an insight on how to go about the soulwinning business. With this, the soulwinner is equipped with adequate information that will help him reach out to the unsaved. When a soulwinner is able to connect current happenings with the message he is presenting to the sinner, the gospel message becomes more relevant and effective.

ABILITY TO PREACH IN SEASON AND OUT OF SEASON

Paul said to Timothy his son in the Lord, "Preach the word; be instant in season, out of season; reprove, rebuke, exhort with all longsuffering and doctrine." (2 Timothy 4:2)

There are two things mentioned in the Bible as not being restricted to time or season. These are prayer and preaching. We are to do them anytime, anywhere. Delay to preach the gospel is very dangerous. Our timely preaching may save a soul from going to hell. Therefore, we must preach in season and out of season, for that is a distinct quality of a good soulwinner.

CONCLUSION

It is expected that a committed soulwinner must be convinced of what he is witnessing. A soulwinner with conviction devotes his time, talents, strength and resources to the furtherance of the gospel. Our conviction about the eternal doom that awaits a sinner, the shortness of time and the urgency of the Great Commission will determine how seriously we take soulwining. Paul said in Roman 1:16, "For I am not ashamed of the gospel of Christ: for it is the power of God unto Salvation to everyone that believeth…" "…I am made all things to all men, that I might by all Means save some." (1 Corinthian 9:22)

CHAPTER 4

THE REWARDS FOR SOULWINNING

"In all labour there is a profit." (Proverbs 14:23a)

When the Standard Oil Company was searching for a representative in the Far East, they chose a missionary to be their representative. They offered him ten thousand dollars; he turned down; twenty five thousand; he turned down it down; fifty thousand, and he turned it down. They now asked, "What's Wrong? He replied, "Your price is alright, but your job is too small, God has called me to be a missionary."

God invested heavily on human souls. A single soul is worth more than the whole world put together. God released His best to purchase the souls of men and therefore He is prepared to pay the best to everyone who works to rescue these souls from perishing in hell. Soulwinning procures heaven's matchless precious reward for the faithful soulwinner. God is faithful and a rewarder of them that diligently seek him(Hebrews 11:6). Seeking Him involves doing His will. Soulwinning is His will and

He pays fabulously for it. In an ideal situation, the size of a worker's pay package should represent the value attached to the work done. God is wiser than man, and He is not unrighteous to forget anyone's labour of love. (Hebrews 6:10).

FAITHFUL SOULWINNERS ENJOY THE FOLLOWING REWARDS:

JOY OF FRUITFULNESS

There is an abundant joy and fruitfulness in service which comes by winning others to t he Lord. No one ever experience the fullness of joy that is in Christ except by laboring to win souls into the kingdom. As heaven rejoices over one sinner that repents, the soulwinner equally rejoices for the harvest. "He that goesth forth and weepeth, bearing precious seed, shall doubles come again with rejoicing, bringing his sheaves with him." (Psalm 126:6) The joy of a farmer is to see his labout rewarded with bountiful harvest. In like manner, the joy of a soulwinner is to see the fruit of his labour in terms of the number of souls won for the Lord. Be a reaper of souls today and experience this joy unspeakable! The joy of a soulwinner is akin to joy of a mother that is just delivered of a baby. It is only right that God will give abundance of joy to a man who makes heaven to rejoice.

OBEDIENCE RINGS BLESSINGS

Nothing brings more lasting joy, peace of mind and blessings in life than obedience to God's commands. The call to the Great Commission—the heart-beat of the Almighty God—when obeyed opens doors of blessings. Blessings of good health, favour from men and success in life endeavours will be the position of any faithful Soulwinner. Testimonies abound among believers that doors of breakthrough opened when they got involved in this work. When a child obeys his father's instruction willingly, it becomes difficult for such a father to refuse the child's request. Likewise, when a believer obeys willingly the Lord's command (especially in this area that is His heart-cry), then He responds positively to the believer's request, soulwinning is a key to answered prayers. The scripture confirms in Isaiah 1:19 "If ye be willing and obedient, ye shall eat the good of the land."

KEY TO GOD'S POWER

Faithful soulwinners experience and enjoy victory and power over the devil. The promised power is for the people who will go out and bear witness for Christ. The seventy disciples who returned from evangelistic outing rejoiced that even demons were subject to them through His name. Jesus testified: "...I beheld Satan as lightening fall from heaven. Behold I give unto you power to trend on serpents and scorpions and over all the power of enemy: and nothing shall by any means hurt you." (Luke 10: 18-19) In this message, Jesus places emphasis on power and victory over the enemy as we go to witness. Many believers lack this power over the enemy because they refuse to evangelize. They have never exercised their God-given right over the enemy.

Many church members are dependent on the pastor for prayers in every aspect of life. Their problem is simple. They cannot exercise authority over the devil because they have refused to go out and preach Christ. Just as no businessman will give a good sum of money to somebody who will not invest this money wisely so it is with God. Great power is reserved for those who work in the field. Satan trembles at sight of any committed soulwinner. "…go ye into all the world and preach the gospel to every creature … And these signs shall follow them that believe; In my name shall they cast out devils; they shall speak with new tongues; they shall take up serpents; and if they drink any deadly thing, it shall not hurt them; they shall lay hands on the sick, and they shall recover." (Mark 16:15, 17-18). What a wonderful privilege! We miss a lot by not being soulwinners. As we witness, power, signs and wonders will follow. Time will fail us to tell of many creative miracles that have followed the preaching of the gospel all over the world.

AVENUE FOR GROWTH

Definite effort for the salvation of others produces testimony of growth and grace. As a soulwinner prays and studies the word, he is given the power to live above sin. God honors his effort and promotes him spiritually. He grows in the knowledge of God. A refusal to win souls stagnates a Christian's growth. To confirm this, one may do a practical check in the church. If you do this, you will discover that most of the brethren that have stunted growth in the church are those who refuse to witness of Christ to others. Such people stay in the church for years but still remain babies in the knowledge and things of God. Such people can easily be tossed to and fro by every wind of doctrine. They are prone to backsliding. Paul captures the essence of this;

> For when for the time ye ought to be teachers, ye have need that one teach you again which be the principles of the oracles of God: and are become such as have need of milk, and not of strong meat (Heb. 5:12)

PURITY

Genuine efforts at soulwinning will help a child help a child of God to remain pure. In other words, preaching the gospel helps to keep one from living in sin. No committed soulwinner will prefer to live contrary to the message he preaches. As he witnesses, he becomes more conscious of the way he lives his life. In the process, through prayer he receives the grace to live a holy life. Compromise with the world is very easy when one refuses to preach. When one gets born again and decides to hide his identity by not letting others know what he believes, such can easily be lured back into sin. The moment he lets people know his new faith, he becomes separated. He is set apart an dno longer joins the wicked to commit sin or do things as before. His feet become "beautiful." No wonder the scripture records in the book of Romans 10:15b, "...how beautiful are the feet of them that preach the gospel of peace, and bring glad tidings of good things!" When one preaches the gospel, his life is daily sanctified. Paul the Apostle said, "For I am not ashamed of the gospel of Christ: for it is the power of God unto salvation to everyone that believeth; ...For therein is the righteousness of God revealed..." (Rom. 1:16-17)

THE SECRET TO PROSPERITY

Apart from other blessings mentioned, witnessing is the secret to material blessing and prosperity. God lifts up His servants materially when they do His work, "...it is the Lord that giveth thee power to get wealth..." (Deut. 8:15) King Jehoshephat prospered above his equals, when he sent teaching priests (evangelists) throughout the land of Judah, to teach the people the Law of God (II Chron. 17:7-9). God is faithful. As we labour in his vineyard as soulwinners. He labours in our own too.

A case study has proven, all things being equal, that those who give generously and joyfully to sponsor evangelism never lack. God is always interested in promoting the business of men who promote the gospel. Try it and God will surprise you.

DIVINE PROTECTION

Soulwinners are fruit bearing trees and they therefore enjoy the protection of God. Jesus testified in Jn. 8:29, "And he that sent me is with me: the Father hath not left me alone: for I do always those things that please the Lord is to win souls. Therefore the assurance is that God will not leave us alone.

Every soulwinner is like a vehicle insured to a reliable insurance company. We are in His hands, much more when we become partners with God in winning souls. Also Jesus assured the disciples as He sent them into the field to reap that the very hairs of their head are all numbered (Matt. 10:30).

DIVINE APPROVAL

God's seal of approval is upon every faithful soulwinner. Jesus said, "Whosoever therefore shall confess me before men, him will I confess also before my father which is in heaven" (Matt. 10:32). Jesus is saying here that as we confess Him before men (witness for Him), He will also talk to the Father about us and about our needs. As we go out to win souls, He will give us divine connection and divine approval!

GODLY WISDOM

Soulwinners are wise Christians. As we witness and interact with people, valuable wisdom to serve God better is gained. Moreover, soulwinning enables us to invest wisely in eternity. People that lack wisdom invest all their resources here on earth. The scripture cautioned, "Lay not up for yourselves treasures upon earth, where moth and rust doth corrupt, and where thieves break through and steal; But lay up for yourselves treasures in heaven, where neither moth or rust doth corrupt, and where thieves do not break through nor steal" (Matt. 6:19-20). Leaving your personal interest is wisdom indeed. Many believers prefer to put their hard earned money into other ventures instead of going out to witness or investing their money in the gospel. Unknown to them, this is good money wasted. Such people will eventually experience huge losses because they lack wisdom. Winning souls is like banking in heaven where earthly inflation, exchanging rate, or economic depressions do not affect the value of our savings. No wonder the scripture says, "...he that winneth souls is wise" (Prov. 11:30).

FRUITFULNESS

Common sense tells us that a farmer will not like to cut down a fruit bearing tree in his farm. Fruit-bearing trees are always the most precious trees in the farm. A soulwinner is a fruit-bearing tree and his life is insured. John the Baptist warned that fruitless trees are to be cut down (Matt. 3:10). Apostle Paul concludes the story, "For to me to live is Christ, and to die gain. But if I live in the flesh, this the fruit of my labour… " (Phil. 1:21-22).

GOOD RELATIONSHIP

Good relationship may develop as a result of soulwinning. A soulwinner is a spiritual parent that gives birth to many children. Relationship always develops between parents and their children. Someone we win for Christ today may be of great help to us tomorrow. Some of us have converts today whom we can joyfully and confidently call our children. In Galatians 4:19, Paul made reference to a group of people as "My little chldrenn, of whom I travel in birth again until Christ be formed in you." He was talking about his spiritual children in the Lord. As a "spiritual parent" he developed a beautiful relationship with them. Such relationship often yield good things. Who can tell? There may be treasure in the mouth of the fish you will catch when you go fishing (Matt. 17:22).

KEY TO ANSWER TO PRAYER

Soulwinning facilitates answers to prayer. The simple truth is that soulwinners have close relationship with God. Simply illustrated, and obedient child is highly regarded and better placed by the Father. Soulwinning promotes responds immediately, "ye have not chosen me, but I have chosen you, and ordained you, that ye should go and bring forth fruit, and that yor fruit should remain: that whatsoever ye shall ask of the Father in my name, he may give to you" (Jn. 15:16).

A close study of scripture quoted above will
reveal the following facts:

a)   We are chosen to go and bear fruit for
       God. This comes through our witness.

b)   We are ordained and anointed by God.

c)   Reason to win souls(bear fruit).

The Lord of the harvest still assures, "...be ye steadfast, unmovable, always abounding in the work of the Lord," (e.g., wining is not unrighteous to forget your labour of love" (I Cor. 15:58; Heb. 6:10). Be a wise investor!

CHAPTER 5

POWER EVANGELISM

"The Spirit of the Lord is upon me, because he hath anointed me to preach the gospel to the poor; he hath sent me to heal the broken-hearted, to preach deliverance to the captives, and recovering of sight to the blind, to set at liberty them that are bruised" (Lk. 4:18)

The gospel of our Lord Jesus Christ is a gospel of power. As we go forth to preach, the Lord works and confirms the word with signs (Matt. 16:20). These signs or miracles that follow the gospel are usually that of mercy from God, and physical proof to the unsaved that God is present with us. Miracles are the manifestations of the supernatural power of God in the lives of men with the aim of attending to their needs and situations. Miracles add color to our witnessing.

Evangelism without miracles is like an unsigned document or a soup that is not well seasoned, miracles, signs and wonders are testimonies unto the unsaved. Sometimes when Jesus performed miracles He would ask the recipient to go and show himself to the high priest for a testimony (Matt. 8:4).

WHO SHOULD PERFORM MIRACLE

Every child of God has the potential to become a miracle worker. It is not an exclusive right of any pastor or evangelist. Jesus confirms that these signs shall follow them that believe (Matt. 8:4). Once we are born again, we are automatically qualified to do miracles. 'But as many as received him, to them gave he power..." (Jn 1:12). This privilege includes power to do miracles, heal the sick, cast off devils and deliver the oppressed.

Jesus, our Master Evangelist, did not only preach, He also performed miracles. The scripture said, "And Jesus went about all Galilee, teaching in their synagogues, and preaching the gospel of the kingdom, and healing all manner of sicknesses and all manner of disease among the people" (Matt. 4:23). Both the early saints and contemporary believers enjoyed the privilege of performing miracles as they preached the gospel. As Christians, it is our turn to demonstrate this God-given privilege.

HOW TO DO MIRACLES

A miracle is not magic; neither can it be imitated. Unbelievers have no portion in it. When Pharaoh's wise men tried to match God's power working through Moses, they could only perform a few stunts. But the rod of Moses--the power of God wallowed up all their little Egyptian idol rods. They could not stand the miracles that God wrought through the hands of Moses and Aaron (Ex. 7:11-12). Simon the sorcerer could only perform magic, but not miracles (Acts 8:9). The seven Sons of Sceva, after witnessing the special miracles of God by the hands of

Paul, desired to cast out an evil spirit. But they could not (Acts 9:11-15).

Miracles do not just happen to entertain people. However, the atmosphere for miracles could be created. There are certain basic requirements and conditions for miracles to take place. Among these are:

Building up faith in Christ Jesus. Motivate and build up the faith to hearers on the word of God. In other words, challenge them to believe what the word of God says, "…if thou canst believe, all things are possible to him the believe" (Mk 9:23. "…according to your faith…nothing shall be impossible unto you" (Matt 17-20). So encourage people to believe God for their miracles.

The attention of the person who will receive the miracle must be drawn to Jesus through powerful, persuasive and positive preaching. Jesus is a miracle worker. He delights in healing the sick, delivering the captives of Satan. As people build faith in the word of God, miracles will take place. The lame man at the beautiful Gate received his healing when his faith was built up. Peter and John encouraged him to look on them. The scripture says, "And Peter fastening his eyes upon him with John, said, look on us" (Acts 3:4). This is to say: concentrate on what we are telling. Receive the word we are sharing with you and have faith that God will heal you. The moment he did that, his feet and ankles received strength and a miracle took place. Put in another way, when the faith of Peter and John clashed with the power of lameness, with the interest of the lame man fixed on Jesus, the spirit of lameness left the man. The end result was the the lame man was "Walking, and leaping and praising God."

DEVELOP YOUR OWN FAITH

We must develop our own faith. As we develop and build up the faith of our hearers, we, on our part must believe God for the miracle. It is possible that an evangelist may encourage his hearers to exercise faith, while on his own part; he may not believe that God can do miracles. Our unbelief can hinder us from performing miracles. The preacher is the faith booster. It is when we have faith that we can speak faith into our listeners. The scripture testified that Jesus did not do mighty works (miracles) in some places because of their unbelief (matt. 13:58). Faith for miracles is developed through prayers, constant reading/hearing of the word of God, and by the power of the Spirit of God.

BE BOLD

As Christians, we need to be bold and courageous and know our right, privileges and our God-given authority without fear. Fear brings a snare (Prov. 29:25). The boldness we are referring to here is the one that comes by the infilling of the Holy Spirit. The source of Christian boldness is the Holy Spirit. We must desire to be filled with the Holy Ghost. From the time the disciples were filled with the Holy Ghost, the timid, illiterate preachers become orators and great workers(Acts 4:13). The Bible testified in that passage that the people took knowledge Peter and John when they saw the boldness in them. People must recognize us when we begin to preach with great utterance, and with signs and wonders. They must recognize that we've gone to the power source (the Holy Ghost) to tap power. Ask God for the anointing. Boldness and anointing make the preacher to possess the gates of his enemies. Joshua, a teacher of the Law, was advised to be so bold and courageous so as to win, gain victory. Hear the admonition: "…be strong and of a good courage; be not afraid, neither be thou dismayed: for the LORD is with thee whithersoever thou goest" (Josh. 1:9). Covet this attribute and witness tremendous miracles in your evangelism.

PRAY AND FAST

It is necessary that we sometimes wait upon the Lord in prayer and fasting, asking God to visit the people as we witness to them. Most of the time, the miracles we see happening in the field have been settles with God in prayers during period of waiting. Prayer and fasting are proven tools to move the hand of God to do miracles. Certain cases will not go unless tackled with prayer and fasting. The disciples of the Lord asked why they sound not do the simple miracle of casting out a devil from a man and got the answer "Howbeit this kind goeth not out but by prayer and fasting?" (Matthew17:21) To demonstrate the need for this indispensable weapon in spiritual warfare, Jesus, on His part, started His earth ministry with fasting and prayer. He also ended it up with strong prayers and tears. A Christian worker desiring to be used by God should seek God earnestly through fasting and prayer. Fasting and prayers reduce the flesh and increase the productivity of the Spirit of God housed in our flesh. Great men in the Bible like Moses, Elijah, Joshua, and Jesus, fasted for many days, to move their ministry up. Fasting and prayer are also necessary in our time so as to move our ministries in the supernatural.

DEPEND ON THE HOLY SPIRIT

God cannot share His glory with any man. Our dependence for the miracles must be upon the Spirit of God. The Holy Ghost is the miracle worker. As Soulwinners, we are only instrument through which the Holy Ghost does the miracles. So we must humble enough to return all glory back to God. The crowd that witnessed the healing of the lame man at the Beautiful Gate were so fascinated by the miracle that they started looking at Peter and John as having great power. Peter had to correct their impression "And when Peter saw it, he answered unto the people, Ye men of Israel, why marvel ye at this? Or why look ye so earnestly on us, as though by our own power, or holiness we had made this man to walk?" (Acts 3:12). If miracles happen during our preaching to the people, we must give God all the glory. If on the other hand, it does not happen immediately, we still must believe God and give Him the glory. As obedient servants, we have done what we are supposed to do; every other thing is God's business. He might decide to heal them after we have left them. Some preachers that are hungry for power employ carnal formulas to fake miracles. They can "push down" their converts to convince them that they have the anointing. This is not what a miracle is all about.

RIGHTEOUSNESS OF THE VESSEL

Holy living attracts the power of God in the life of an individual or evangelist. So, before any evangelist begins to seek to perform miracles, such a person must be a child of God who is living right with God. Anointing to do miracles is for those living holy lives. Holiness and righteousness is not optional for any believer who wants to be used by God for power evangelism. The difference between workers of fake miracles, signs and wonders, and genuine miracle workers is righteousness and holiness. The devil cannot fake holiness because he cannot afford to be righteous or holy. He may appear as an angel of light, but eventually his true evil nature will be manifest to all.

Vessels of honor are the Master's use. Apostle Paul admonished Timothy, the young evangelist thus: "if a man therefore purge himself from these, he shall be a vessel unto honour, sanctified and meet for the Master's use and prepared unto every good work." (2 Timothy 2:21)

COMPASSION FOR THE VICTIM

Compassion provokes holy emotions in the heart of the preacher, making him want to help. When we have concern for someone's problem, we will pray more to God asking Him to take care of the problem. Instances abound where Jesus healed the sick as a result of the burden and love He had for the victims. The Scripture confirms this: "And Jesus moved with compassion, put forth his hand, and touched him, and said unto him, I will, be thou clean. And as soon as he had spoken, immediately the leprosy departed from him, and he was cleansed." (Mark 1:41-42) When we have compassion, we put on the nature of God (who is the embodiment of compassion). This makes the performing of miracles easy as we pray for the recipient.

DESIRING TRUE SPIRITUAL GIFT

Possessing spiritual gifts is very important When we have spiritual gifts, miracle and deliverance prayer becomes easy. Spiritual gifts help the evangelist to locate the problem of the people easily. This will help him to deal with the need of the recipient's situation appropriately, when the gifts of wisdom, working of miracles, and faith operate in a man, time is saved because he knows where the problem is and tackles it straight away.

It is good to desire spiritual gifts, and it should be the heartbeat of all Christian workers. The scriptures has a standard for those desiring to be used by God.

> "If a man therefore purge himself from all these, he shall be a vessel unto honour, sanctified, meet for the master's use and prepared unto every good work."
> (2 Timothy 2:21)

If a man purge himself from the affairs of this life, works of the flesh, and all iniquity and defilement, the person's desire to be used can be actualized and maximized.

THE IMPORTANCE OF MIRACLES

Miracles are great assets to the Gospel preacher. The saying that "action speaks louder than words becomes appropriate when miracles are involved in our preaching. It silences every doubt in the heart of the seeker and brings quicker conviction. These are numerous cases of people who have repented as a result of miracles the received.

Miracles are also proof that Christianity is a living gospel.

It makes the gospel real quick and active. When John the Baptist's disciples came to inquire whether Jesus was the Messiah or not, the Lord used the miracles that He performed to prove His point to them. He told them, "…go and show John again those things which ye do hear and see: the blind receive their sight and the lame walk, the lepers are cleansed, the deaf hear, the dead are raised up, and the poor have the gospel preached to them." (Matthew 11:4-5)

CHAPTER 6

THE PLACE OF THE HOLY GHOST IN EVANGELISM

"And behold, I send the promise of my Father upon you; but tarry ye in the city of Jerusalem, until ye be endured with power from on high" (Luke 24:49)

It must be emphasized from the very beginning that evangelism is a battle fought And won in the spirit realm. The "going forth" to win souls is to encounter the opposing forces. The Lord never allowed any disciple to go forth without equipping him with power and authority. He commissioned the twelve disciples and gave them power against unclean spirits, to cast them out, to heal all manner of sickness and all diseases.(Matthew 10:1) God knows that to get the work done effectively, we need divine assistance through the Holy Spirit. The best, the most eloquent and logical preaching may sound nice to people but their hearts will remain dead until the spirit comes to create life. Miracles, signs, and wonders are possible when the Holy Spirit is involved. Opposition arguments, resistance to the gospel melt into oblivion when we are in partnership with the Holy Ghost. "For the people shall be willing in the day of thy power…" (Ps. 110:3)

Below are some of the works of the Holy Spirit in Soulwinning:

DIRECTING THE HARVEST

The Holy Ghost is the chief witness. God is raising a great end-time army of harvesters by His Spirit. The Holy Ghost knows best the condition of the harvest and the urgency of the work. He recruits, trains, and sends laborers into the field. Jesus said, "Pray ye therefore the Lord of the harvest, that he will send forth laborers into his harvest." (Matthew 9:38) The Holy Ghost knows the right instrument to use in His harvest. The issue is not that there are no laborers, but that qualified ones are very few. People who love the Lord and His work are very few. People who love the Lord and His work are scare. God cannot use unqualified vessels for the harvest no matter the need. If companies will not employ just anybody to occupy important positions, the Lord of the harvest will not either. The Holy Ghost supervisors to ensure that the right materials are selected for his harvest. Our duty is to pray and the Holy Ghost will do the selection. God only told Ezekiel to prophesize and the Holy Spirit will raise a great army from dry bones (Ezekiel 37:4-10). It is the Holy Spirit who gets us enlisted for the job.

EMPOWERMENT OF THE LABORERS

UTTERANCE

The Holy Ghost empowers and equips the soul winner. What to say, and how to say it, depends on the enablement of the Holy Ghost (Acts 2:4). Looking at this verse, it is

very clear that utterance comes from the chief witness. He enables the speaker to say what the mind of God is for the hour. He brings the word of knowledge and word of wisdom. He brings the word of knowledge and word of wisdom. He brings the correct interpretation to the scriptures. Utterance cannot be gotten by mastering the art of sermonizing. The one hunch read and twenty disciples in the upper room become mighty speakers after the Holy Ghost descended upon them. In just a day, three thousand souls were won to the Lord by preaching of Peter (Acts 2:41). The door of utterance is very important to any preacher. Among other things, Paul requested the
Philippian saints to pray for him asking: "…that utterance may be given unto me, that I may open my mouth boldly, to make known the mystery of the gospel." (Ephesians 6:19) Utterance by the Holy Ghost brings out the mystery of the gospel and makes the sinner tremble. Felix the Governor could not withstand Paul as he preached with great utterance under the power of the Holy Spirit (Acts 24:25).

BOLDNESS

When a preacher is endued with the Holy Ghost, holy boldness will come. Fear and lack of courage will disappear. When the timid, uneducated disciples received the Holy Ghost Pentecost, there was a dramatic change in them. The hitherto discouraged and disillusioned disciples, who clustered together in fear in the upper room declared the gospel with boldness. Peter and John spoke so powerfully and boldly that the people marveled. The account of this is recorded in I Acts 4:13, "Now when they saw the boldness of Peter and John, and perceived that they were unlearned and ignorant men, they marveled; and they took knowledge of them, that they had been with Jesus." People will have no option than to listen to the preacher when he is preaching under the action of the Holy Ghost. The reason why many are bored with the gospel is that there is no action and boldness coming from the ministry.

POWER, ANOINTING, AND MIRACLES

The Holy Ghost supplies the power and anoints the preacher for miracles. The anointing makes the difference between one preacher and the other. Evangelists with the anointed by the Holy Ghost, he speaks words that bring salvation and transformation of life. Genuine anointing and miracles follow evangelism as a proof that Jesus is alive. People will look for us when we have what the need. Great multitudes followed Jesus when they beheld the miracles that were done (Matthew 4:23-25).

ACTIVATION OF THE WORD

The spirit of God breathes upon the word and makes it active. The Holy Ghost puts life in the word we preach. The message will remain dead as long as it is not quickened by the Holy Ghost. "It is the Spirit that quickened; the flesh profiteth nothing, the words that I speak unto you, they are spirit, and they are life." (John 6:63) When the word is activated, it removes doubt and creates conviction, and this leads a sinner to repentance and salvation. This happened on the day of Pentecost when the Holy Ghost activated the word in the month of Peter. When the people heard Peter's preaching, they were cut to the heart and asked, "Men and brethren, what shall we do?" (Acts 2:37) Paul testified to this, 'For our gospel came not unto you in words only, but also in power, and in the Holy Ghost, and in much assurance…" (1 Thessalonians 1:5)

The story is told of a particular brother who began to witness as soon as he got saved. One day he followed the brethren, for evangelism. But because he was new in the fellowship, and had not known much, he kept asking the sinner he met, "Where will you spend eternity?" This was all he knew to say. But because the Holy Ghost quickened this question in the heart of that particular sinner, he did not sleep at night. The next day he traced this particular brother to his home; and surrendered his life to Christ. The word was activated by the power of the Holy Ghost.

THE HOLY GHOST PURIFIES

The Holy Ghost is a cleansing agent. He purifies and transforms lives. He brings deep conviction in the lives of sinners that makes them cry out for salvation.

HE CONVICTS AND CONVERTS

Jesus said, "And when He (the Holy Ghost) is come, He will reprove the world of sin, and of righteousness, and of judgement." (John 16:18) It s the Holy Spirit that brings conviction and conversion in the heart of the unsaved. Essentially, this is the power that leads the sinner to repentance and salvation. During ministration of the word, one's heart may begin to burn strangely. This happens when a sinner is pricked in the heart to start asking, "What shall I do to be saved?" When this happens, such a person is said to be saved?" When this happens, such a person is said to be under the conviction of the Holy Spirit. The

Holy Spirit breaks through the hardest heart. The keeper of the prison where Paul and Silas were kept was compelled to believe I faith of his prisons because of the wonder-working power of the Holy Ghost. The problem in the Church is that there are men and women who never at any time got convicted of their sins, hence they not mean conversion. A change of Church does not mean conversion or salvation. We need to allow the Holy Spirit to convict us so that we can be converted to Christ.

He sets the tempo for evangelism Holy Ghosts is the initiator of evangelism. The first thing any preacher must seek is Holy Ghost. He is the first condition to be met before our evangelism becomes effective. When one is born again, there is a measure of the spirit given to him. The Bible says, "…as many as received him, to them gave his power to become the sons of God." (John 1:12) A believer with this initial experience can still preach the gospel, but the baptism in the Holy Ghost is necessary for much result and effectiveness. The Holy Ghost knows the nature of harvest very well and He takes His position in the battle by first filling the saved with His presence so that they can now move into the field. Jesus advised the disciples to wait to be filled with the Holy Ghost before going out to witness. The Holy Ghost therefore is the "vehicle for evangelism."

HE SORTS OUT OBSTACLES

The Holy Ghost sorts out obstacles in evangelism. In most places, the gospel is resisted because of the activities of evil spirit and satanic powers. These evil powers are working through many culture and social system to close the doors to the gospel in many communities. Satan blinds the mind of the people in order to hinder them from being saved (2 Corinthians 4: 3-4). Resistance and opposition may come from the government. Occult influence can also threaten the entrance of the gospel to the particular area.

The devil may also instigate and bring hatred and division between the churches and the evangelists. These are examples of some of the obstacles which the Holy Ghost can handle. By the spirit of discernment, this area of problem is identified and dealt with in prayers. Paul, filled with the Holy Ghost (the Spirit of discernment) was able to know that Bar-Jesus was manipulating the faith of the Deputy, Sergius Paulus from receiving the gospel (Acts 13:7-10).

Without the spirit of discernment, the evangelist may not identify problems easily. He may not know when he steps into the territory of the enemy. He may mistake strange spirit for the Spirit God. In Acts 16:16-18, as Paul and his missionary team went to pray, a girl possessed with the spirit of divination identified with them. In fact, she became a self-appointed "public relations officer" for Paul for many days. She continually announced that Paul and his team were, the servants of the Most High God who came to bring to them the way of salvation. Though her information was true, it was from the wrong spirit. Paul quickly identified the evil spirit by the by the help of the Holy Ghost. He rebuked the spirit of divination and the damsel was set free. This saved the Church from the confusion that the evil spirit would have brought.

HE CHOOSES THE VESSEL
The Holy Ghost selects the vessel in evangelism. He

knows the right person for the work at every point in time. The Spirit of God knows who is suited for what job. For example, the Holy Spirit specifically directed that Paul (Saul) and Barnabas should be anointed and separated or consecrated for special assignment. "As they ministered to the Lord, and fasted, the Holy Ghost said, separate me Barnabas and Saul for the work whereunto I have Called the them" (Acts 13:2).

From the old to the New Testament, the Lord chooses His vessels. God chose Jeremiah from his mother's womb. He chose Paul to carry the Gospel to the Gentiles. The scripture reports:

"But the Lord said unto him, Go thy way: for he is a chosen vessel unto me, to bear my name before the Gentiles, and Kings, and children of Israel." (Acts 9:15)

The Lord decides whom to use in any generation. There are still many vessels yet unsaved whom the Lord will callat the appointed time. Our duty is to evangelize. Even our converts may be the vessel God will use for this generation.

HE CHOOSES THE FIELD

The Holy Ghost also chooses the area for evangelism. He knows the need in the different area. The Holy Ghost knew the need in the city of Macedonia and chose Paul to go. This is one area where many preachers are disobedient to the Holy Spirit. Today the Holy Ghost may be persuading many evangelists to go the villages for evangelists while they prefer to stay in the cities. A close look at the scripture reveals that the early disciples were obedient to God and accepted their postings. By the leading of the Holy Ghost, Peter went to Caesarea to minister to Cornelius and His household (Acts 8:25-26). Today, some evangelists choose to go even when the Holy Spirit is directing them elsewhere.

HOLY GHOST DEFENDS

When the Holy Ghost sends, He defends. Satan hates soulwinners because most times they dispossess him of his captives. The devil does everything to harm the evangelist but God always providing protection. By the power of the Holy Ghost, idols and charms are destroyed. By the same power, His servants are protected from any attack. The Holy Spirit defends the church from anything that can ridicule the gospel. In fact, whenever the devil poses a challenge, God will always rise to defend His name.

In a particular church, the pastor was ministering on a Sunday morning when two young ladies came into the church. The pastor did not know that they were agents of Satan sent from the marine world to attack him and through the church into confusion. But as these ladies settled down and the pastor began preaching, the Holy Ghost gave the pastor a song to sing. Before he could finish the song, the Holy Ghost lifted the first girl up and dropped her halfway to the alter.. The second girl stood up to run but was caught by the vigilant ushers. The girls later confessed that their mission was to kill the pastor.

HE DIRECTS AND ENLIGHTENS

During evangelism, the Holy Ghost enlightens the

preacher. Philip moved to join the Ethiopian Eunuch on his chariot by the Holy Ghost directives. Left on his own, he would not have dreamt of joining a moving chariot. They Holy Ghost knew that the Eunuch had a need—to have the gospel expounded to him so that he would be saved. Today, many have one need or another and God by His Spirit directs us to minister to them. The Holy Ghost reveals and englightens the soul winner on the mysteries of the word of God.

Whereby, when ye read, ye may understand my knowledge in the mystery of Christ: which in other ages was not made known unto the sons of men, as it is now revealed unto his holy apostles by the Spirit (Ephesians 3:4-5)

THE NEED FOR THE HOLY GHOST IN EVANGELISM

What soul winners need most is to be continuously filled with the Holy Ghost so that they will reap tremendous harvest. The early Apostles saw this great need and when Paul got to Ephesus, the very first thing he asked the twelve disciples which believed was, "Have you received the Holy Ghost since you believed?" (Acts 19:29). It was with these twelve, after being baptized in the Holy Ghost that the whole nation of Asian was turned "upside down" for the Lord. Within a space of two years, the region then known as with mere human methods, formulas, strategies, and eloquence alone? God is in need of Spirit-filled believers who will do exploits in evangelism. The harvest is plenteous but the laborers are few. We need the Holy Ghost to be worthy laborers in His vineyard.

CONDITION FOR HOLY GHOST OUTPOURING

Many have tried in their "Jerusalem" (presence of God) to be endured with power from on high for long and God invariably visited them with His power! Some others are still shopping around for the best carnal methods to do the work. The truth is that heaven is waiting for us to come and be filled.

To qualify for the Holy Ghost's outpouring we need:

To be genuinely born again (John 3:3)

To absolutely surrender to God

To seek the glory of God

To thirst for the power of God (Matthew 5:6)
To be pure in heart and live
(Mathew 5:8)

To exercise faith that will bring the fulfillment of the promise.

CHAPTER 7

PRAYER WARFARE IN EVANGELISM

"For we wrestle not against flesh and blood, but against principalities, against powers, against the rulers of the darkness of this world, against spiritual wickedness in high places." (Ephesians 6:12)

Evangelism involves battles – several battles to deliver souls out of the clutches of Satan, out of captivity, oppression, and darkness into freedom, light, and joy of the Lord God. In it, the soul winner aims to dispossess and subdue the devil thereby enforcing his rights and privilege in Christ. Consequently, Satan will mount a formidable force to oppose both those who want to give their lives to Christ and the soul winner. The ultimate aim of the devil is to keep the unsaved in their condition, keep off the soul winner, and eventually drag such unsaved souls into hell. Satan employs various tactics to frustrate the conversion of sinners and the effort of the soul winner. It can be through false religion, evil traditions, culture, worldliness, diverse kinds of bondages, and manipulations. As Satan hinders souls from being saved, he also keeps the soul winner busy with the cares of this world and other distractions.

NECESSITY OF PRAYER WARFARE

No evangelist will succeed without prayer warfare. Preachers will remain ordinary men, and messages will remain mere speeches. Sinners will remain impenetrable to the gospel until prayer warfare is carried out to checkmate satanic forces. Otherwise how can one enter a strongman's house without first binding the strongman? (Mathew 12:29) The onslaughts of satanic forces against evangelism are a pointer to the fact that the task of soul-winning is important to God. That is why our prayer warfare has to be aggressive.

The peculiarity of this warfare is that physical weapons are not needed. "For though we walk in the flesh: for the weapons of our warfare are not carnal, but they are might through God to the pulling down of strongholds." (2 Corinthians 10:3-4) Therefore, to fight this battle of snatching souls from the grip of Satan successfully, the assistance of the Holy Ghost is imperative

THE ROLE OF THE HOLY SPIRIT IN PRAYER WARFARE

He helps us to pray as we ought. The Holy Spirit is the potent agent in prayer warfare. He directs operations as soul winners pray. It is therefore necessary that evangelists desire to be filled with the Holy Ghost so that the warfare because easy. The scripture makes it very clear that the Holy Spirit helps us to pray right "…for we know not what we should pray for as we ought: but the spirit itself maketh intercession for us with groaning which cannot be uttered." (Romans 8:26) As we pray, the Holy Spirit goes ahead of the evangelist to prepare the ground.

EMPOWERMENT

In prayer warfare, Holy Ghost empowers the evangelist to move to the field and humble the enemy. Areas that appear not penetrable initially with the gospel will yield when we pray through the Holy Spirit. He does this through convictions, miracles, signs, and wonders. When the power comes, souls will be willing to repent. "The people shall be willing in the day of your power…" (Psalm 110:3)

Nature of prayer Warfare in Evangelism God has bestowed upon soul-sinners important weapons especially in rescuing the souls of men. The prayers that get souls saved are not just prayers offered carelessly. Such prayers must be:

Born out of a heart burdened for the lost (Lamentations 1:12): When the heart of a soul winner is charged with this type of prayer, he will cry that all the barriers that hold men from repenting will collapse and that the hearts of men be melted and broken to receive the gospel.

Constant, consistent, and persevering (Luke 18:1): The evangelist or team of soul winners who pray like this will not take "No" for an answer. They keep on praying, breaking Satan's yoke over lives of men because they believe firmly that the door for the gospel must be opened. Difficulties and discouragements from sinners, communities, or authorities are challenges broken by persevering prayers.

Challenging the forces of darkness (Daniel 10:12-13):

Here the soul winner aggressively challenges the prince and the powers controlling the land. Many villages, communities, and cities are being held bound by traditions, ancestral forces, deities, and spirits. Unless these forces are dealt with, the gospel will not penetrate. Therefore, the activities of these forces in holding souls captive must seriously be contested in prayer warfare just as Daniel did. Daniel's prayers defeated the prince of Persia.

Accompanied with Fasting (Matthew 17:21): Some stubborn forces that withstanding the evangelists in the field and detain the souls of the unsaved may not give way unless they are given the quiet notice by prayer warriors who know how to legislate in the realm of the spirit through prayer and fasting. Sometime ago, some brethren made two attempts to organize an evangelistic crusade in a particular area but they were beaten and drove away on those two occasions by the natives. The brethren decided to go into two weeks of prayer and fasting and pray purpose fully to break into the community. After sometime strange things began to happen in this community and the leader of the area invited the same people they drove away to hold a crusade there. At the end they handed over the town to Jesus.

Prevailing, wrestling, and agonizing (Acts 16:25-31); Luke 22:41-44): This type of prayer, is done in evangelism, opens closed doors, unlocks the heart of the unsaved and magnifies the Lord whom the evangelist is serving.

WEAPONS OF PRAYER WARFARE

It is both encouraging and greatly heartwarming to know that the weapons of warfare are at our disposal are might through God and are capable of containing the satanic activities that oppose our efforts at getting men saved. These weapons arm the soul winner to step into the enemy's territory.

OFFENSIVE WEAPONS

Word of God: Such weapons include the Word of God or the word of faith. When spoken in faith and in prayers, it shatters the stronghold of the devil. No wonder the Lord Himself retorted, "Is not my word like as a fire…and like a hammer that breaketh the rock in pieces?" (Jeremiah 23:29) Moreover, soul winners overcome by the confession of the Word, "for they overcame him by the blood of the Lamb and by the word of their testimony…" (Revelation 12:11)

The Blood of Jesus: this armor serves for offence and defense. When applied the devil has not option than to bow. There was a case where some Christians spent hours just pleading the blood of Jesus on a particular town they wanted to evangelize. When they eventually went, they came back with testimonies of less opposition and great number of sinners turning to Christ. The blood of Jesus van also be used to protect the preacher against any arrows of the devil while in the field. The scripture declares…when I see the blood, I will pass over you." (Exodus 12:13)

The name of Jesus is a great offensive and defensive weapon. At the mention of the name of Jesus, every knew, of things that are in heaven, on earth and beneath the earth bows (Philippians 2:10). The Master Himself asked us to use His name to knock out Satan. "…in any name, shall they cast out devils…" (Mark 16:17)

The testimony of the saints in an offensive weapon as well. Our word of testimony makes Satan a liar and bears witness that God has been and will continue to be our deliverer. "And they overcame him...by the word of their testimony..." (Revelation 12:11)

DEFENSE ARMOR
Apostle Paul listed some of these weapons:

1. Lions girt about with truth

2. Feet shod with the preparation of the gospel of peace

3. Breastplate of righteousness

4. Shield of faith

5. Helmet of salvation

6. Praying with all prayers in the Holy Ghost

7. The sword of the Spirit, which is the Word of God

ANALYSIS
Helmet of Salvation: This is the first requirement for a soldier of Christ to be enlisted into spiritual warfare. You must have testimony of salvation first to protest yourself from demonic bullets directed at the mind. Satan seeks to control the mind and use it to operate effectively. This is why the Bible admonishes us to keep our mind fixed on Christ (Colossians 3:2, 2Peter 3:2).

The Breastplate of Righteousness: Keeps the evangelist

from the fiery darts of the enemy. By both preaching and practicing righteousness, you will keep Satan's accusations away, and the Lord will uphold you in your integrity.

Belt of Truth: The believer must be sure he believes in the thing. False belief will fail in prayer warfare. The Word of God is truth and sufficient, no more, no less. Moreover, we must live lives of truth, without falsehood.

The Sandal of Preparation of the Gospel: This armor of God gets the evangelist on the move to go out for practical evangelism. God out in the field where the sinners are and prepare yourself to look like the gospel you preach.

Shield of Faith: Faith gives security to the preaching evangelist from all the arrows of Satan. If God be for us, who can be against us?

Prayers: Prayers have no distance problems. You can fight, intercede, and pray all manners of prayers as one of your weapons of war.

The Sword of the Spirit: This is the Word of God which is for both offense and defense. It is like to a sword. The armors are meant to defend the evangelist against the attack of the enemy. When applied in spiritual warfare, they have the potency to serve as a covering and protection for the evangelist from any harm.

The devil might rise up after souls are won, idols in the land are destroyed, or even charms are burnt to attack the evangelist. The armors then become a protective device. Cases also abound where the enemy will try to draw the new converts back, but those weapons will be used to battle against the devil until victory is won.

There are several miracles of salvation, healing and deliverances in the Bible as a result of the use of spiritual weapons in prayer Warfare (Acts 2:37-42, Acts 4:4).

TYPES OF PRAYER WARFARE
BINDING THE SRONG MAN:

"Or else how can one enter into a strong man's house, and spoil his goods, except he first bind the strong man and then he will spoil his house" (Matthew 12:29)

There is no doubt that the strongman referred to here is Satan. The spiritual rope or chain for binding Satan is prayer warfare. The goods to spoil which he has are the souls of men. The evangelist must set Satan's captives free.

Every evangelist who knows his calling must spend quality time to bind and disarm the enemy in prayers before going to the field for evangelistic programs. There are an organized network of evil government, headed by Satan. Proper knowledge will lead the evangelist to constant prayer warfare to destroy and dislodge their plans. However, we will always depend on the Holy Spirit to perfect our warfare. We must not allow ourselves to fall to the delusion of attributing everything to the devil, thereby magnifying him instead of God who is in charge of everything, including the devil.

ROOTING OUT AND PLANTING
We are God's battle-axe (Jeremiah 51: 20-25). We are His instruments of warfare. God wants to use us to root out all satanic forces that hinder the salvation of men. He also

wants to use us to plant righteousness and good works I the lives of men.

SPIRITAL MAPPING

Spiritual mapping is an instrument of prayer warfare Proper knowledge of the gods in the land, the occultic level, and major shrines in the land will help the evangelist know what to battle with. Geographical location of each object of worship in the land opens the eyes of the evangelist to know what strategic position to assume or take in order to deal an effective blow to the devil. The topography of the land and the socio-cultural and socio-political life of a city are all necessary for both evangelistic activity prayer warfare.

FAMILY AND LAND DELIVERANCE

This is another level of prayer warfare. It is true that some evangelists have misunderstood the principle of family and land deliverance. Yet, the fact still remains that most African communities and traditional families were dedicated to one form of a god or another. This explains why in this part of the World people still bear names that are associated with idols and shrines peculiar to their families. Family generational history is a strong history that will help the evangelist to lead those affected to denounce the covenants with those gods. Evangelists who are knowledgeable in carrying out deliverance must break these chains and lead those families to Christ and prayer of faith to set them free. They should be asked to hand over their land to God to attract God's glory and favor. Lastly, they should be linked to God's new covenant thought the blood of Jesus "...the earth is the Lord's and the fullness thereof..." (Psalm 24:1).

RESULT OF PRAYER WARFARE
We can achieve tremendous result though warfare prayer if we pray by faith.

OPEN DOORS:
When we are in prayers, utterance and boldness to proclaim the gospel is received. Apostle Paul requested brethren to pray so that this door of utterance be granted unto him (Colossians 4:3, Epesians 6:9). When this door is opened, mysteries of salvation will be spoken and the hearts of many will yield to the truth. The gospel becomes irresistible to the hearers.

MASS CONVERSION OF SOULS (Acts 2:37-41):
When serious prayer warfare is made, scales in the eyes of men removed. The heart of men can now be pierced by the Word of God. Men will without argument, yield to the gospel and begin to ask, "What shall we do to be saved?" That was the case in the days of the Apostles (Acts 2:37).

LESS OPPOSITION:
With effective prayer warfare, the opposition against the gospel will minimize. Those who were hostile to the gospel will begin to yield to the gospel. When prayer is used to wet the ground of communities, their strong men will surrender to Jesus Christ. There have been instances where entire communities surrendered their gods and idols for destruction. Others abolished the observance of demon-

inspired customs and cultures. These are made possible by reason of aggressive prayer warfare.

Miracles, signs, and wonders become a common phenomenon as prayers are made towards evangelism. Rooting out evil and planting righteousness in villages, towns, and cities by the power of gospel is accomplished. Curses and covenants are broken and land, families, and people freed when we overcome the devil through prayer warfare.

EXAMPLES OF PRAYER WARFARE

People who wage war through prayer in the Bible days obtained tremendous results. In Acts 12:105, the Bible records that Herod the King persecuted the church. He killed Apostle James and dumped Peter in the prison. It was then that the church woke up to her responsibility. They worked in prayers to stop further threats from King Herod and to secure the release of Peter from the prison. The Bible said, "Peter therefore was kept in prison: but prayer was made without ceasing of the church unto God for him." (Acts 12:5) This particular prayer warfare by the church threw open the formidable prison gates and sets Peter free. God can still do the same for us today if we pray.

Jesus, the Master-Evangelist, and our supreme pattern engaged in such aggressive prayer warfare before His crucifixion. Consequently, it was said of Him, "And being in an agony he prayed more earnestly: and his sweat was as it were great drops of blood falling down to the ground." (Luke 22:44) No wonder, the devil could not withstand

His victory at the cross of Calvary.

Elijah also prayed earnestly that it should not rain and for three and half years, and it was so (1 Kings 17:1).

These are just a few instances in the Bible. There still exist a long list of men and women who engaged in prayer warfare for a particular purpose and God honored it. They prevailed in prayer and moved the hand of the Almighty God to do the impossible. The lists include:

Abraham (Genesis 18:23)

Jacob (Genesis 32:24)

David (Psalm 55:17)

Hezekiah (II Kings 19:15)

Esther (Esther 4:16)

Daniel (Daniel 6:10), etc.

Today, the Lord has appointed us as chosen instruments to reconcile the world unto Himself (2 Corinthians 5:19). We have been commissioned to be soul winners. We can be another Elijah to bring about a great harvest of souls in this end time. We will prevail through warfare prayers.

CHAPTER 8

EFFECTIVE WITNESSING

"That which was from the beginning we have heard, which we have seen with our eyes, which we have looked upon, and our hands have handled of the word of life; …we have seen it and bear witness…" (1 John 1:1-2)

EFFECTIVE WITNESSING BY COMMITTED SOUL WINNERS

Prior to any effective witnessing, there must be an experiential personal knowledge of the events, actions, and situation by the one so testifying. A very reliable witness is that given by somebody who saw, heard, and touched the subject matter. Apostle John is said to be an effective witness of the word of life because he had these facts (1 John 1:1-2). Effective witnessing is always focused and targeted, and produces a result-oriented evangelism.

Witnessing is judged to be effective when:

1. Christ and His Kingdom is message.

2. The end result is conversion.

3. The Convert is turned into a witness also.

The noblest profession approved by heaven is living a holy life and witnessing to win souls for Christ. This is a faithful saying and worthy of all acceptation.

Of course, we know that this was the first and last commission of our Lord Jesus Christ. To the first group of people who Christ chose to be his disciples, He said, "Follow me and I will make you fishers of men." The last group who followed Him to his ascension received this command, "Go and make disciples of all nations."

Jesus himself was a sour winner. He commissioned His first disciples also to win souls and by this, they became the first witnesses of the Lord Jesus Christ. Effective witnessing refers to the methods, strategies, principles, and conditions that will accelerate soul-winning and discipline. It involves a concise, precise, and targeted message leading to conversion of souls. God purposed that our soul-winning must be rewarded with concrete results. This leaves us with no alternative than to do all we can to become effective in the business of soul-winning and win souls that will abide.

Below are some of the elements of effective soul winning:

1. THE MESSAGE DESIGN

Our Message should carry the plan of salvation, in a simple manner that the sinner will understand. It should be precise, concise, and targeted to lead a soul conversion.

The aim of the message is to challenge, inspire, and motivate a sinner to surrender his life to Christ. Simply put, the message is, "...all have sinned, and come short of the glory of God" (Romans 3:23). "For God so loved the world, that he gave his holy begotten Son, that whosoever believeth in Him should not perish, but have everlasting life." (John 3:16) God therefore demands repentance from sin, and faith in Christ Jesus, in order that sinners may be saved(Acts 3:19). The message is not that of condemnation(John 3:17). Deviation from this simple gospel presentation is defective. Every gospel message must center on Christ and His coming kingdom.

The message is not just intended to arouse the interest of individual so as to make him become interested in attending a particular church (Luke 6:46) or to make him change his denomination (Acts 4:12), or even to become religious (Isa 64:6). The message should be aimed at convicting and converting a sinner by making him discover his helplessness without Christ. The eyes of the sinner should be opened to the sufficiency of the finished work at Calvary, which Jesus so as to be able to make a decision the end result is for him to forsake his sins and receive Christ as his personal Lord and Saviour.

The packaging of the message should be direct, simple, and sincere. It must include the following:

a. The lost state of man

b. The recovering drive by God through Christ(that is the gospel)

c. The only option left for man is to accept God's remedy(His salvation)

d. The consequences of ignoring God(the wages of sin)

e. The blessing of knowing and serving God

2. ADOPT A METHOD

Effectiveness in soul-winning begins with using the right method for the right person at the right time. This could also be referred to as strategy for effective witnessing. A witness must be tactful to be able to draw the sinner into discussion on the subject of the gospel. It is important that the soul winner get the attention and the interest of the person his is ministering to. The approaches can be classified into two:

A. Direct Approach(question method or simple request)

In this approach, the soul-winner introduces the theme of the message at the outset. This direct approach (or question method) may be used as a leading from the Holy Spirit, or due to limited time before the evangelist. The soul winner may still like to get a direct answer. Examples of such direct question are: "Are you born again? Where will you spend eternity? Do you know that Jesus loves you?"

In applying a direct question method, caution must be applied. The soul winner should introduce the question in a cautious and polite manner to avoid provoking the listener: Otherwise, this could close the door to the gospel. John the Baptist's message to the Pharisees and Sadducees who came in his days for baptism was "...repent ye: for the kingdom of heaven is at hand (Matthew 3:2). The Holy Spirit led him to begin this way. Sometimes as people go to witness we hear comments like "Go I will not like to listen to you." The reason may be due to wrong approach.

The direct approach could be in the form of a simple request: Please may I speak to you about the Lord Jesus Christ? Or Please may I share with you briefly on the hope of eternal life which God has provided in Christ? Such a simple request often opens great doors of opportunity to witness.

B. Indirect Approach

Indirect approach is another way of approach the sinner and gaining his attention to the gospel. This involves starting a conversation on current social happenings that are of interest to the sinner before directing his attention to scriptures. This leads the person from the physical to the spiritual truths and gradually builds up his convictions to yield to the gospel. The method used by Jesus to minister to the Samaritan woman could be referred to as an indirect approach. He first began the conversation on her area of interest by saying, ",,, give me to drink" (John 4:7). This drama eventually led the woman to salvation. Paul also makes use of this method in Athens, a city given to idolatory. He approached them by strategically preaching to them about the God they referred to as "the unknown God." For effective witnessing, the soul winner should depend on the Holy Spirit for Wisdom on the best approach suitable for a particular situation.

C. Tract/Literature Approach

This involves the use of well-written track or gospel materials to witness to the sinner: These are normally given out to sinners to create an opportunity for discussion on the subject of salvation. In some cases, letter-writing and even projection of gospel films may be used in soul winning.

There is, however; no hard and fast rule about a particular formula. The approach adopted depend on the type of evangelism, time constraints, the situation on the ground and the leading of the Holy Spirit.

3. OVERCOME INHIBITIONS

There are several things that could inhibit or limit our effectiveness as soul-winners. Below are some:

A. Inferiority Complex

This is one of the many complexes that could impede our effectiveness in soul-winning. It could in various forms. Some feel they are not qualified: others feel they are not eloquent (like Moses of old). All these should be done away with. Excuses of not being eloquent, or of not occupying a high position in the society should be done away with. Excuses of not being eloquent, or of not occupying a high position in the society should be overcome. God is not after all these as He is not a respecter of man. He can use anyone who is willing.

The soul winner should be conscious of the fact that he is a witness, and carries a priceless message – all have sinned and therefore everybody needs salvation. The commission the soul winner received is to preach the gospel. Inferiority complex is a tool which the devil uses to hinder the soul winner especially when the level of education is low. But the soul winner will do well to remember when he meets the so called elites that the Holy Spirit is there to give the required strength and wisdom. We have an assurance from the Bible of the help and presenc of the Holy Spirit, (Psalm 119:99-100). The Apostles were described by the elites as "… unlearned and ignorant men…" (Acts 4:13), yet they bore a powerful witness and that changed their generation.

B. Personal Limitation

An effective witness should overcome every personal limitation. Lack of good education, physical disability or other limiting factors may pose a problem to a soul winner. One can update his knowledge by further study and become literate.

The disabled should also know that there is ability in disability. Physical disability can be converted to God's ability. With God there is no limitation.

A well-known Christian sister was paralyzed to such an extent that she could not move. Yet she was able to win souls through letter writing. Physical disability should neither be an impediment nor an excuse. Moses was a stammerer yet God used him to deliver the Israelites out of Egypt. You can equally be used to reach others.

C. Satanic Blockade

Often, there are satanic blockages that hinder effective witnessing. Paul told the Corinthian brethren that "… a great door and effectual is opened unto me, and there are many adversaries" (Corinthians 16:9). In this case, we need to deal with these satanic hindrances that close the door of the gospel. We must root them all out through prayer and fasting.

4. DIFFERENT TYPES OF WITNESSING

There are two major types of witnessing: Normally, the type to be chosen depends on:

- The Audience

- Time Factor and

- The distance between the evangelist and the recipient.

These two major types of witnessing are:

a. Mass Evangelism(Acts 20:20a)
b. Personal Evangelism

MASS EVANGELISM

This may take the form of a crusade, organized and advertised in the electronic or print media, using posters, banners, etc. In this case, the work is shared in departments, while one evangelist will minister to the large crowd. Great evangelists like Dr. Billy Graham (a great American evangelist) and Reinhard Bonnke(a German Preacher) use mass evangelism to reach out to millions of souls at a time.

Church or Temple Type Witnessing (acts 5:42)

This type of witnessing is also mass evangelism. It is an indoor crusade where people are reached with the message of salvation. It was widely used by the apostles, "And daily in the temple, and in the every house, they ceased not to teach and preach Jesus Christ" (Acts 5:42).

EPISTORAL OR LETTER WRITING

This type of witness can be used for either mass or personal evangelism. The Apostle Paul used this extensively. He wrote to single individuals as well as to congregations. Such letters are biblically worded and written to encourage, exhort, rebuke, or minister salvation to a person or group of persons. It is necessary to use this method when the recipient is far from the evangelist.

Other types of mass evangelism include television, radio, internet, etc.

PERSONAL EVANGELISM

This method of evangelism or witnessing is very reliable. This involves person to person, house to house, street to street witnessing aimed at bringing souls to Christ. It was commonly used in the Bible by the following:

Jesus to Nicodemus (John 3:1-12); to the Samaritan Woman (John 4:7-26); Philip to Ethiopian Eunuch (Acts 8:27-39); Paul to Felix(acts 24:24-27).

This method brings us face to face with the convert and gives the convert the opportunity to ask questions after discussions.

TRACT OR LITERATURE WITNESSING

Where distance or time hinders the soulwinner from giving a detailed message, tract or literature witnessing works better.

This is normally done by choosing and sending a tract or a good Christian book in the subject we want the convert to read.

5. PRACTICAL HINTS FOR EFFECTIVE WITNESSING

a. Before going into the field

PRAYER: A soulwinner should devote a good time to prayer before venturing in to the field. Neglecting prayer before preaching cannot make for a successful preaching.
As mentioned in the early part of this book, evangelism is warfare. The soul winner should therefore war to subdue the gods of the land before moving out to preach

(Matthew 12:29). The scripture says, "I will give thee the heathen for thine inheritance, and the uttermost part of the earth for thy possession" (Psalm 2:8).

The soul winner needs to remember that the person to be preached to belongs to another kingdom and to bring such a person out requires passing the gate of his keeper (Satan) and binding him. Pray for boldness and break the walls of unbelief so that the hearers will believe the gospel.

PREPARATION: this necessary since the soul winner cannot know for sure the person he will meet. Since he could meet a witch doctor or an occultist, he must therefore be sure of the anointing of the Holy Spirit.

The soul winner will also need to pray for Compassion(Romans 9:1-5). Paul had a great compassion for his people of Israel. A compassionate heart will move us to speak the Word of God and the Holy Ghost will confirm it with signs and wonders.

Live an Exemplary Life: A soul winner must not live a dubious life, as this will hinder his message. Our lives speak more than what we say. Therefore, a soul winner should endeavor to live by examples in order to create a lasting impact on his hearer. Paul admonished Timothy, "…but be thou an example of believers, in word, in conversation, in charity, in spirit, in faith, in purity" (1 Timothy 4:12)

SPEND TIME TO STUDY THE WORD:
Knowledge, they say, is power. Therefore, the soul winner should study to avail himself of adequate knowledge of the word of God. Our audience must come to appreciate our

understanding of the subject of discourse. They must have confidence in the message we are preaching. To achieve this, adequate study and preparation in the Word of God is the answer. A soul winner must not live under the assumption that God will provide the right words to speak once he opens his mouth, if he has not spent time on God's word. It is careless living and a lazy man's approach to witnessing. Paul's advice to Timothy is "study to show thyself approved…"(2 Timothy 2:15).

6. HINTS IN THE FIELDS

During the course of sharing the gospel with sinners, the target of the soul winner is to win souls for Christ. Therefore, proper care must be taken to say the right words and to put up the right behavior so as to achieve the desired aim. The following, if followed, would be helpful:

BE FRIENDLY: The prospective convert could feel uneasy if the soul winner looks too serious of unfriendly. It is therefore necessary that the soul winner try to put up a cheerful disposition and introduce himself politely to the prospective convert or audience.

BE HUMBLE: Thee soul winner must not show any sign of superiority. We are all sinners saved by grace. The main focus of the outing is Christ Jesus. Humility and good behavior will attract the sinner to the message of the soul winner.

DO NOT PREACH DEMONINATION: Any preaching or attack on any denomination or doctrine is a deviation from the core message of salvation. The soul winner must preach Christ and Him crucified.

PERSERVE: The soul winner must spend more time on people who respond to his message, but must not give up so soon on any sinner. He must speak and preach with faith and authority.

BE ALERT IN THE SPIRIT: The soul winner must be in a prayer mood to sharpen his sensitivity.

EMPHASIZE CHRIST: The emphasis must be Christ and the gospel, not on the soul winner.

AVOID UNNECESSARY QUESTIONS AND ARGUMENTS: The soul winner must not allow the sinner to keep him business with unnecessary questions and should not enter into argument with the sinner. The biblical injunction is that we be wise as serpents and harmless as dove (Matthew 10:16). Learn to navigate to your central focus – Christ!

BE DECENT: The soul winner should look neat and decent. Offensive odor and dressing could repel the prospective convert (1 Corinthians 10:32).

WATCH THE STORIES YOU TELL: The soul winner must avoid telling sad stories while witnessing. Point the sinner to Christ (1 Peter 3:19). Get them to make a decision for Christ. The sinner must not find it easy to postpone the decision to give his life to Jesus.

AVOID CLOSE RELATIONSHIP WITH THE OPPOSITE SEX: The soul winner must avoid unnecessary closeness to the opposite sex while witnessing. He should avoid any emotional overtures from the prospect.

DO NOT LOSE HOPE: The soul winner must leave the discussion open ended so that it could be revisited any other time. He must not lose hope when the result of his witnessing is not what he had expected.

7. THE PURPOSE OF A GOOD MESSAGE TO A SINNER MUST INCLUDE THE FOLLOWING:

All have sinned. A good message to a sinner must be targeted to bring our listeners to understand the fact that all men have sinned and so every man needs repentance. Others may choose to present their self-righteousness, saying how religious they are, but the soul winner presents the word of God. He includes himself as a sinner, but is saved purely by God's grace.

Behold, I was shapen in iniquity, and in sin did my mother conceive me (Psalms 51:5)

For all have sinned, and come short of the glory of God (Romans 3:23)

SIN HAS A PENALTY:

For the wages of sin is death; but the gift of God is eternal life through Jesus Christ our Lord (Romans 6:23)

This death is "the second death" (Revelation 20:14). It is death in hellfire, and is final, without hope of a future deliverance.

This message brings the punishment of sin in focus and a suggestion of a way of escape. The penalty of sin is sure but the soul winner's work is to present the way out. This is the good news.

Present God's Love to the Sinner:

…Who will have all men to be saved, and come unto the knowledge of the truth (1 Timothy 2:4)

God is God of love and not condemnation. As said earlier, our message is not that of damnation but love. It was love that brought Christ to the earth to die for all of us. God's love must be emphasized to the people.

Jesus Paid the Penalty of Sin:

But God commendeth his love towards us, that while we were yet sinners, Christ died for us (Romans 5:8)

This is agape love. He died for us when we still hated Him. Jesus died to pay for our sin. The duty of the sinner is to believe.

Faith is needed for Salvation: That if thou shall confess with thy month the Lord Jesus, and shall believe in thine heart that God has raised Him from the dead, thou shall be saved (Romans 10:9)

Faith is imperative; and a crucial stepping stone to salvation, while salvation also opens the door to sonship and receiving from God.

Search for and Expose the Hiding Place of the Listener: Practical experience in the field has shown that would – be converts can easily find things to console themselves with, so as to delay their salvation. Some believe that God is too good to punish sin. People who reason like this think that God can condone sin. They say, "God is not a kill joy. He is so good that He cannot send any sinner into hell." The work of the soul winner is to make them understand that God's mercy and love cannot be spurned forever. He waits patiently until death, and once the person dies judgment in the death of a sinner.

Some believe that their sins are so many that they cannot be forgiven. Again, tell them that there is no sin that God cannot forgive them. The soul winner should make the converts know the power in the blood of Jesus. Forgiveness is available for all sins unless when the sinner dies in his sin, after which the sinner cannot repent.

Others believe that there are too many errors in the Bible and would not want to believe since they are not sure of the part the Bible that is correct. This philosophy is upheld by those who insist that the Bible is the word of men. The Bible itself contains proofs of its authentication.

Jesus said, "...the scripture cannot be broken" (John 10:35).

> Knowing this first, that no prophecy of the scripture is of any private interpretation. For the prophecy came not in the old time by the will of man: but holy men of God spoke as they were moved by the HOLY GHOST (2 Peter 1:20-21)

Still others believe that if they are doing their best, everything should be alright. To this group, godliness is a matter of personal effort. The soul winner should make them understand that our effort is not needed. God in the person of Jesus, has finished it. It is our duty to believe it. There is a standard set by God. That standard is only attained by accepting Jesus who is the righteousness of God.

Other still believe that there is no life after death. "So why worry about life after now" they ask.

This is erroness. Man is made up of a spirit, soul, and body. We leave the body at death to pass into another life, either in hell or in heaven. The story of the rich man and Lazarus in Luke 16:19-31 makes this very clear. Man was created in the image and likeness of God. As such, he is a living soul. A soul does not die but continues to live after leaving the flesh. The question to pose to them is "where will your soul spend eternity?" Every man must answer that question correctly.

CHALLENGE THE FAITH OF THE PEOPLE TO LEAD THEM TO CHRIST:

A motivational word is that a soul need to lead him to action to confess and decide for Christ. The soul winner should lead sinners to confess their sins after all is said and done. Pray for them and assure them that God has forgiven them on true repentance. They should then be introduced to a good fellowship within their neighborhood.

Although it is important to witness, it is however, more

important to witness effectively. Effective witnessing requires knowledge, wisdom, and demonstration of the power of God. The soul winner must endure hardness as a good soldier and preach in season and out of season (2 Timothy 4:1-5). This will bring a fruitful result to the glory of God.

8. EVIDENCE OF EFFECTIVE WITNESSING

Witnessing must be done in such a way that there will be tangible results. When evangelism is effective, the fruit will abide. That is the ultimate desire of our Lord when He said in the scripture "Ye have not chosen me, but I have chosen you, and ordained you, that ye should go and bring forth fruit, and that your fruit should remain..."(John 15:16).

When soul winners carry out the task effectively the result is usually a qualitative and bountiful souls – harvest. This is the desired fruit that soul winners should produce for the kingdom of God. When our witnessing is thorough, and Bible-centered, we produce converts that are well grounded in the Word, who stand firm in the Lord, and grown in grace. The soul winner should withhold nothing that will be profitable to the sinner during witnessing. Paul testifies, "And how I kept back nothing that will be profitable unto you, but have showed you, and have taught you publicly, and from house to house"(Acts 20:20).

Some people today are witnessing with wrong and ulterior motives. Such people present the gospel in a way that will enable them to achieve their purpose. They often hide from the sinner the consequences of sin and eternal judgment because they want to make easy converts and big crowds. Some will emphasize prosperity at the expense of holiness and righteousness. Such preaching gives false security to the sinner. The Lord warned the Pharisees of the danger of converting a proselyte (a Gentile convert of Judaism) and making him "twofold" and the child of hell (Matthew 23:15). We, too, must beware of this error.

Effective witnessing demands that we preach the full gospel as it is written in the Bible. The message must not be bent to suit anybody's taste.

CHAPTER 9

FOLLOW-UP IN EVANGELISM

"And when they had preached the gospel to that city, and taught many, they returned again to Lystra, and Iconium, and Antioch, confirming the souls of the disciples, and exhorting them to continue in the faith and that we must through much tribulation enter into the kingdom of God(Acts 14:21-22)

WHAT IS FOLLOW-UP?
Many believers have done the work of evangelism in many ways, but the souls won were lost because of inadequate follow-up. Lack of follow-up can be likened to a fisherman catching a fish, and then letting it fall back into the water instead of killing it and putting it in the boat.

The procedure adopted by soul winners to establish the new convert in the faith and bring them up in the knowledge of the Lord is what we refer to as "Follow-up."

THE IMPORTANCE OF FOLLOW-UP

Our evangelism responsibility is grossly incomplete if the new converts are not followed-up. Preaching the gospel to sinners constitutes the first phase of a soul winner's work. Nurturing or following-up is the second phase of the work. The essence of follow-us is to achieve the following:

a. Produce Genuine Converts

Follow-up helps the soul winner to produce genuine converts. Some of the problems that church members have today could be n traced to inadequate follow-up after conversion. If the soul winner labors to win a soul and allows that soul to go back to sin due to inadequate follow-up, he lacks understanding of the real essence of soul winning. A soul winner therefore cannot proudly say he has made converts until such converts are properly followed-up to maturity. It is only a lazy hunter that will neglect to kill and roast the animal caught during a hunting expedition. A diligent man(hunter) would regard his substance as precious (provebs 12:27)

Those who follow up their converts value their souls. They are precious to them and cannot be toyed with. In fact as it is negligence of the highest order for a mother to abandon her baby, so it is for a soul winner to abandon his converts and fail to follow up properly. This was why Paul and Barnabas decided to go back to Antioch to confirm the state of the souls that had been won for Christ and to establish them in the faith (acts 14:21-22).

b. Product Disciples

We are born to reproduce ourselves. Christian life and maturing comes in stages. The nned for follow-up is to enable the converts to become grounded and genuine believers and followers of Jesus Christ (disciples), who in turn will reproduce other disciples.

c. First Contact May Not Lead to Salvation

Since this is true, follow-up therefore becomes necessary to further persuade the convert to make up his mind. Repeated visits to the new converts will make them open up to share their challenges and struggles with the soul winner.

d. An Unwelcome Visitor May Take Over If Follow-up is Delayed

If an evangelist delays in the follow-up of the new converts, the devil or his agents may take him over again. This is because soul winning is a battle between the kingdom of God and that of Satan. Normally, the devil is not happy to let go of his captives. This is why he will do everything possible to bring the soul back. So, it is not just doing a follow-up that is the issue, but doing it in good time – as soon as the souls are won. Time must not be lost between the time the sinner makes a confession of faith in Jesus and the follow-up to block the devil from countering what has been done.

There was a case of a woman converted from one of the cults. She gave her life to Christ, but as Christians delayed her follow-up for over two weeks, she relapsed as her old friends and members visited her. This happened because Christian brethren neglected doing their follow-up work on time. Christians generally, and soul winners in particular, should learn to stand by their converts to get them grounded and establish in faith, especially at the time of persecution, of course, once the convert makes a decision to follow Christ, the person who led him/her to Christ becomes their only true friend at that moment.

e. Rooted in the Faith

Follow-up helps the new converts to stabilize in the faith and be established in the Word of God. It gives the convert a sense of belonging and makes him know his right as a child of God. Besides, follow-up can be a veritable tool in restoring backslidden Christian as repeated visits and encouragement will strengthen and build up their faith.

Through follow-up teachings, a new convert will become strengthen in God's Word, and be able to withstand temptation which follow conversion.

f. Fulfilling the Lord's Command

Our Lord and Savior Jesus Christ emphasized the imperative of follow-up in the following words:

> Go ye therefore, and teach all nations, baptizing them in the name of Father, and of the Son and of the Holly Ghost: Teaching them to observe all thing whatsoever I have commanded you...(Matthew 28: 19-20)

'Teaching them to observe all things" refers to follow-up exercise. The disciples were charged to teach those who responded to the gospel "to observe all things" that Christ commanded in order to establish them in the faith. Even Jesus Christ, our role model in evangelism, after witnessing in the city of Samaria, tarried for two days with converts to do follow-up with them (john 4:39-40).

BIBLICAL EXAMPLES OF FOLLOW-UP

Paul, an effective soul winner, followed up his converts, visiting, teaching, and praying with them. At a time, Paul likened his follow-up activities to travailing mother wanting to give birth. This he said he would do until "Christ is formed" in his converts (Galatians 4:19). At another time he told Barnabas, "...Let us go again, and visit our brethren in every city where we have preached the word of the Lord, and see how they do."

METHOD OF FOLLOW-UP

There are various methods of following a new convert. The right method is that which the soul winner wisely considers as most appropriate at the point in time. All the methods are aimed towards nurturing the young convert in the faith. Some of these methods are:

PRAYER: Once the battle for a soul is won, effective prayer is required to keep the soul of the new convert. The soul winner does this aggressive prayer warfare to consolidate the new convert who has just been snatched from the jaws of hell and from the Kingdom of Satan. Through prayers, the soul winner will dislodge every attempt by the enemy to take the soul back. The necessity of prayer is informed by the fact that most times we meet people we preach to while on transit. Since prayer is not limited by distance, we can pray and believe God to establish them in the faith.

VISITATION: Times visitation of the new convert is of utmost importance. It is not proper for a soul winner to neglect visitation and leave his soul winner visits to provide, care for and comfort the new convert in the way of the Lord. Such visitation also brings the soul winner closer to the new convert.

CONSTANT TOUCH: Then a soul winner is strictly indisposed to go, he can still keep in touch with converts through phone calls or letter writing. Communication has been made easy modern technology. Many new converts have gone back to the world because they lost contact with their spiritual parents. When the converts are denied regular encouragement and comfort, they may backslide.

GOOD CHRISTIAN MATERIALS: Good Christian literature and magazines with a letter encouraging the convert to read them could be resource materials for building up the new convert if he is literate. Audio and video tapes can also be sent to the convert if available.

PRACTICAL LOVE: A warm practical love shown in cash and kind is a potent tool to follow-up a new convert; it quickly builds relationship and fellowship. Caution, however, must be exercised in this direction to avoid being misunderstood (especially when dealing with the opposite sex) or building the faith of the convert on material things rather than the Word of God. But in all, practical love is important. A brother once confessed that he lost a convert because he was unable to help him out of financial need, and the amount involved was relatively small. We must show practical love and assist our converts when they are in need.

INVITATION TO FELLOWSHIP: Efforts must be made as soon as possible to expose the new converts to the fellowship of brethren. This is an important aspect of follow-up. Interaction into the family of believers and build his faith quickly.

Failure to do this could be likened to a woman who delivered a baby refusing to take her baby home. This is the foolishness of the wild ostrich (Job 39:13-18). Fellowship exposed the new converts to a new environment, new friends, and new understanding of the reality of heaven. While doing this, the soul winner has a duty to explain to the new convert anything that may be regarded as a strange happening in the fellowship. For example, in a tongues speaking fellowship, it would be necessary to explain the new phenomenon to the new convert, backing it up with the scripture. Otherwise, the new convert could give any interpretation to it and may not inform the soul winner when he makes up his mind to leave the fellowship.

TESTIMONY: The soul winner should make time to share his testimony with the new convert especially the testimony of his salvation and that of others, and later encourage the converts to share the testimony of his own salvation in the fellowship. This will help him make proper separation from the old life to live the Christian life. The Bible rightly says, "They overcame him by the blood of the

Lamb and by the word of their testimony" (Revelation 12:11)

WISDOM TIPS IN FOLLOW-UP: Ensure that follow-up is done as quickly as possible. Unnecessary delay I doing this could result in the new converts losing the initial zeal. It is good not to keep off for months before visiting the new convert (Acts 15:36)

Show love, patience, and tenderness to a new convert just as a nursing mother will show to her baby. Begin by feeding the new convert with the sincere milk of the word of God. Care must be taken not to expose the new convert to "bones" (hard doctrines) prematurely (1 Peter 2:2).

Encourage and appreciate the little personal testimonies of the new converts. Though they may be small, your readiness to listen attentively and to encourage the 'baby's" new steps of progress would go a long way to strengthen the faith of the converts (Zechariah 4:10).

Listen to the new converts and identify their areas of needs and problems. The problems of a new convert could be social, spiritual, or doctrinal. In all, the willingness to pay attention to their problems is vital to enable the soul winner to counsel and pray appropriately for or with them.

Maintain a cheerful disposition before your converts, but not when he has fallen back into sin. In that case, the soul winner must be firm to make the new convert understand and see the dangers of meddling with sin. The new convert should be restored in love. The soul winner should remain courteous and friendly.

PERSEVERE: The soul winner must not give up or get discouraged by the initial failures of the new convert. Like a baby, the new convert is not expected to grow up and become an adult in a day. Handle the new convert with love and wisdom.

Caring must go beyond their physical welfare. Ask about their health, business, and family. This leaves a good impression on the hearts of the new convert.

THE SOUL WINNER'S RESPONSIBILITIES TO THE NEW CONVERTS

There are basic things that a soul winner is expected to teach the new convert as part of the follow-up exercise. Listed below are some of them.

Teach him how to pray in faith according to the promise of God (Matthew 7:7-11, 1 Peter 5:7).

Teach him how to live the new and victorious Christian life (1 Peter 2:1).

Teach him to develop the daily habit of studying the Word of God (Acts 17:10-11)

Encourage him to share his testimonies (john 1:40-46)

Teach him the necessity of Christian fellowship. Show an example by bringing him to the Church for worship and fellowship (Hebrews 10:25).

Teach him practically how to live the Christian life by your own example.

Teach him the basics of the Christian life: salvation, repentance, promise of God, authority of a believer, faith in Christ, obedience, etc.

Teach him to obey the Great Commission – witnessing (Matthew 28:20)

Encourage him not to listen to the voice of the devil who tries to deceive him that he is not born again. The devil sometimes ministers evil thoughts in the heart of the new convert to make him doubt his salvation (2 Corinthians 5:17).

HOW NOT TO FOLLOW-UP

The period of follow-up is a serious learning process for a new convert. How a soul winner should do the follow-up therefore becomes very important. Some of his actions can make or mark the life of the new convert. Below are some of the "Don't" a soul winner must avoid.

Do not burden your converts with your personal problems; rather be a solution to his problems.

Do not make promises to the new convert you cannot keep. This will bring distrust. He looks up to you as a spiritual model and any double standards can destroy his faith.

Do not ask your converts for financial help. Remember, money is a deep sea where honor, conscience, and truth may be drowned. Protect the image of Christ that you carry.

Do not assume or pretend to have, all the answers to all his questions. Refer to your pastor or other mature Christians who are knowledgeable enough to help when and where necessary. It is better not to answer the new convert's question at all, than to give the cover wrong answers.

Do not visit the opposite sex at odd hours of the day or in secret places. Avoid unnecessary closeness that can lead to suspicious and sin.

Remember, the eyes of all in the neighborhood are watching you.

Do not date your converts (opposite sex).

FRUITS THAT ABIDE

Follow-up which is the second phase of evangelistic efforts should never be neglected. It is not enough to win a soul, but to get such a soul rooted in the faith is much more important. Just as is attainable in real life, after a baby is born; clothed, fed, taught to crawl, walk, and so on. Most times, this involves money, time, energy, and sleepless nights, but the joy of it all is that a baby is brought up in the family. This is exactly what follow-up can be likened to. How can the fruit abide if we do not follow-up the converts? In John 15:16, Jesus said "Ye have not chosen me, but I have chosen you, and ordained you, that you should go and bring forth fruit (win souls), and that you fruit should remain."

The only way the fruit will remain is through follow-up.

AMEN

REFERENCES

1. Osborn, T.L., 1966: Soulwinning Out Where the Sinner Are, Osifo Publications.

2) Dake Annotated Reference Bible, 1998: USA (fourth printing).

3). God's World Christian Ministry Thursday Bible Study Outline, 1999.

REACHING THE TARGET IN SOUL WINNING

God's World Christian Ministry (GWCM) Inc. was founded in Maryland, USA in 1994. The vision was given by the Holy Spirit to facilitate the work of evangelism through the mobilization of Church congregations for soul wining.

It is my prayer that the Holy Spirit will impart the fire of evangelism into the hearts of everyone that reads it.

AMEN

Bishop (Dr) Godfrey K. Tabansi

Other Books by Bishop Godfrey K. Tabansi

1. Guiding Your Children Into Their Destiny

2. By Prayer and Fasting

For any information, comments and/or if you would like
to reach Bishop Tabansi, please contact us at:

Divine Publishers Inc.
www.divinepublishersinc.com
Email: divinepublishersinc@gmail.com

Notes